Bonin

INTRODUCTION

With hundreds of plants available for your garden, the challenge is choosing the best ones for your site. Some need lots of sun and others thrive in shade. Some can sustain a drought, while others need regular watering and feeding. Like the cardinal rule of real estate, the three most important considerations for plants are location, location, location.

The approach we took in this book—placing plants in their proper habitats—is one that's used extensively in Europe and becoming popular in this country. There, as well as here, gardeners who carefully consider location for their plants are more likely to be delighted with the results of their labors.

Many Granite State gardeners have asked the question we set out to answer in this book: What plants grow best in New Hampshire gardens? We've assembled a stellar team of writers (see page 97 for more about them), who share their many years of experience to give you their best recommendations.

Our writers have selected some of their favorite plants for each habitat and provided helpful information on them in the text as well as in easy-to-use charts. These charts also include other plants our writers recommend. Take advantage of our writers' expertise—in the habitat sections as well as in the lists they've compiled for using plants in your garden, starting on page 80—and try some of their favorite plants, which are available at most garden centers.

If you haven't already discovered this for yourself, we warn you that gardening gets under your skin. In the introduction to her book, *My Favorite Plant*, renowned writer and passionate gardener Jamaica Kincaid says, "A garden, no matter how good it is, must never completely satisfy. The world as we know it, after all, began in a very good garden, a completely satisfying garden—Paradise—but after a while the owner and the occupants wanted more."

Here's wishing you the garden you've always wanted—and more! We hope this book helps you work smarter in your garden.

—AA

TABLE OF CONTENTS

PART I

The Seven Habitats

Bonin

Bonin

WOODLAND AREAS

Woodland areas can be as small as a grouping of trees near the house or as large as a mature woodland or park. In spring, when sunlight shines through tree branches and moisture from rain or melting snow abounds, certain species thrive before tree leaves emerge and cast shade on the underplantings. That's when attractive ferns, spring-flowering bulbs, and some perennials take center stage. Species that thrive in woodlands have to tolerate shade, withstand competition from tree roots, and grow in soil rich in woodland humus.

Read on to learn more about some of our writers' favorite plants for Woodland Areas. And refer to the chart that follows for details on bloom time, light requirements, and more for these plants and others our writers recommend.

Favorite Annuals for Woodland Areas —MH

Baby-Blue Eyes (Nemophila menziesii)

This shade lover has deeply cut, gray-green leaves that are topped with clouds of bell-shaped, upward-facing flowers in shades of blue and white. A stunning bloomer in late spring and early summer, baby-blue eyes can fade a bit during extremely hot summers. The dainty, blue flowers are also attractive in sunny meadows, rock gardens, mixed borders, and containers.

Browallia, Bush Violet (Browallia speciosa)

Browallia, or bush violet, has a different texture and different flower colors than impatiens, but can be used in all the same places (woodlands, beds, borders, and containers). Its growth habit is bushy and upright, and the flowers are approximately the same size and shape as impatiens but with a different appearance. If you're looking for an underused shade plant that's easy to grow, this could be it.

Lobelia, Edging Lobelia (Lobelia erinus)

Lobelia has narrow leaves and two-lipped tubular flowers that come in dense, rich colors. Most often used as an edging plant or in containers and hanging baskets, lobelia is a knockout early in the season. Unfortunately, it has a habit of drying out and dying in hot summer weather. Shear it back in mid-summer or plan to have other plants crowd it out as they reach their full potential.

Tuberous Begonia (Begonia tuberhybrida)

The huge, lush, and beautifully defined flowers of tuberous begonias look almost surreal. Fortunately these showy plants are easy to care for—all they require is a cool, shady location. Stems are thick and succulent (occasionally brittle) and the handsome, angel-wing shaped foliage comes in either green or bronze. Male flowers are fully double and female flowers are single (you may want to pinch these off as soon as you see them so the plant's energy goes into producing the showier male flowers). Tuberous begonias make a handsome edge, are showy in mixed borders, and do well in containers.

Wax Begonia (Begonia semperflorens)

Massed together in deep shade, wax begonias provide a spectacular display. Individual plants have little impact, but put a group together and it's a totally different story. Wax begonias have a round shape and small flowers. They are a true workhorse, blooming abundantly from planting until frost. Foliage is green, bronze, or occasionally variegated. Wax begonias make a nice ground cover, edging plant, mixed border, or container plant.

Favorite Perennials for Woodland Areas —LvB

Alkanet (Brunnera macrophylla)

Alkanet resembles a forget-me-not but with large, dark, textured leaves (eight-to-10 inches wide if they're happy). The big leaves make a wonderful contrast to the tiny blue flowers, which are a true blue (rare in the perennial world). Alkanet is good for borders, massing in groups, and can take some dry shade. If it is planted too far north, often the mother plant will die, but seedlings will take over.

Barrenwort (Epimedium rubrum)

One of my favorite choices for a dry woodland site, barrenwort is a choice semi-evergreen ground cover known for graceful, heart-shaped foliage and columbine-like flowers (flowers arise before the leaves). Barrenwort does well in dry conditions under trees and in deep shade, spreads vigorously but not invasively, and the leaves are on wiry stems that make it tremble in the wind like an Aspen tree.

Bugbane (Cimicifuga racemosa)

This standard woodland native is a great architectural specimen perennial with tall, spectacular airy spires of white flowers in late summer. The foliage is divided and gives a fine texture, and the whole plant has a lovely form, which is almost Japanese-like. If given a moist site, it will fill a four-foot space. Bugbane's only drawback is that its flowers don't smell very good, so keep it away from your windows. You can give it quite a bit of sun, as long as it doesn't dry out.

Tuberous Begonia

Wax Begonia

Creeping Phlox

Bunchberry (*Cornus canadensis*)

A pretty little spreading native dogwood with small white flowers and scarlet fruit, bunchberry requires moist, acidic soils with lots of humus. It's a great ground cover in wooded areas with tall pines, mountain laurel, and rhododendrons, which require similar conditions. Bunchberry is expensive but impressive when massed in large numbers.

Canadian Wild Ginger (*Asarum canadense*)

Canadian ginger is a woodland native that should be used more often. It has large, heart-shaped, "eggshell-satin" leaves that make a lovely, bold-textured ground cover. Canadian ginger combines well with other wildflowers, tolerates dry conditions, and is especially good to cover bulbs or other plants that go dormant by mid-summer.

Creeping Phlox (*Phlox stolonifera*)

This woodland phlox is a unique evergreen ground cover that forms a mat of attractive rounded leaves. Flowers rise high above the foliage but fade gracefully (which means no deadheading). There are many different cultivars on the market in shades of purple, pink and white, and they can be interplanted for a tapestry effect, although the white forms generally disappear after a few years. Creeping phlox does best in moist soil and is wonderful naturalized among other woodland perennials or under shrubs and trees.

Crested Iris (*Iris cristata*)

Crested iris is a pretty, miniature iris with strap-like leaves that can be used as a woodland ground cover. It doesn't form a weed smothering mat, so it's best interplanted with other wildflowers. The flowers are small, but exactly like larger irises, so this can appeal to those of us who love tiny things. Crested iris is very adaptable, but is best in fertile soil with some sun each day.

Ferns

There are many native ferns to choose from and their fine feathery textures make them the ultimate shade foliage plant. Most do best with even moisture and part shade. Ferns either creep with underground rhizomes or stay in a cluster – your local garden center should be able to tell you which ones they have. Choose ostrich or cinnamon fern for a large statement, or Japanese painted fern or maidenhair fern for a different look. They are lovely when contrasted with some of the large-leafed shade plants, such as ligularia or hosta.

Foam Flower (*Tiarella cordifolia*)

Foam flower is a textured maple-leaf ground cover for the woodland. It has light green leaves and long-lasting "foamy" flower spikes that light up a dark corner of a wooded site. The flowers go by very gracefully, never needing deadheading, and it will spread quickly and even crawl over low items, such as logs. *Tiarella* is easy to care for and has many cultivars available, with varying leaf shades and colors.

Fringed Bleeding Heart (*Dicentra eximia*)

One of the most popular shade perennials with pendulant, heart-shaped flowers and finely textured foliage, this bleeding heart blooms for many weeks,

Siberian Barren Strawberry

Redvein Enkianthus

TOWER HILL BOTANIC GARDEN, BOYLSTON, MA

Doublefile Viburnum

beginning in spring, unlike the larger old-fashioned bleeding heart. It is fast-growing and easy, and produces many seedlings each spring.

Grapeleaf Anemone *(Anemone tomentosa 'Robustissima')*

Many woodland plants bloom in the spring, yet this anemone is a stunning fall bloomer, with large, single, pink blooms, and textured grape-shaped leaves. Grapeleaf anemone prefers rich moist soil, and will form colonies very quickly. Give it a large area to fill in zone 4 or 5 (central or southern New Hampshire).

Hosta, Plantain Lily *(Hosta varieties)*

One of the great garden foliage plants, hostas produce bold textures in the landscape and will take dry shade. Their large leaves are wonderful contrasted with ferns, *Dicentra*, and other fine-textured shade plants. Some of the large ones, like *Hosta sieboldiana,* will form magnificent specimens. All can be planted in large groups as a ground cover, even though most are clump forming. Almost impossible to kill, hostas are rugged and long-lived, and you can find many different sizes, shapes, and leaf variegations. Their only problem is slugs—try a scratchy mulch or diatomaceous earth to discourage them from climbing on.

Labrador Violet *(Viola labradorica)*

This *does* grow in Labrador, so it is very hardy and durable, although it looks very delicate with dark, purple-tinged tiny leaves and miniature dark violet flowers. It will quickly form a ground cover and retains the best purple color in the leaves if it has some sun. A lovely underplanting for shrubs in the woodland, Labrador violet reseeds very readily.

Lily-of-the-Valley *(Convallaria majalis)*

This is one of the old-fashioned, classic ground-cover perennials, with sweet-smelling, bell-shaped flowers and wide, strap-like leaves. It forms a mat very quickly in all conditions except dry soil. Don't plant it with delicate small plants, because they will be "run over" by this pretty ground cover. Plant lily-of-the-valley in a large drift and have a spring wedding—its sweet smell will intoxicate the whole party.

Siberian Barren Strawberry *(Waldsteinia ternata)*

I feel this is an under-used perennial, related to New Hampshire's strawberry plants but much more ornamental. Siberian barren strawberry is a compact and lush ground cover with evergreen leaves, and is covered with bright yellow flowers in the spring. Often used in graveyards or in sites that get little maintenance, it is drought-tolerant, non-invasive, and a good spreader.

Sweet Woodruff *(Galium odoratum)*

Sweet woodruff is an easy ground cover with delicate, star-like foliage that makes a soft and fine texture under trees or shrubs. It's perfect for woodland plantings, even tolerating "maple-base dry zones" with loose fertile soil. It has hay-scented foliage and is considered an herb. Its historic name is "ladies bed-straw," and is thought to be one of the plants that the mother of Christ rested on. Sweet woodruff has tiny white flowers in spring that resemble snowflakes and is very vigorous, once established.

Favorite Trees and Shrubs for Woodland Areas —CN

Carolina Rhododendron (*Rhododendron carolinianum*)

With an open and airy growth habit, this evergreen rhododendron should be used in a naturalized woodland setting. Three-inch flower clusters vary in color from pink to lilac-rose or pure white, all pale shades that brighten up the shaded woodland when in bloom.

Doublefile Viburnum (*Viburnum plicatum* var. *tomentosum*)

This is a very graceful, horizontally branched shrub. It is beautiful all season, with large, white flowers, dark-green "pleated" leaves, wine-red fall color, and bright-red fruit that birds love. The cultivars 'Mariesii,' 'Shasta,' 'Marie's Doublefile' or 'Pink Beauty' are preferred for their heavy flowering, fall color, and scarlet berries. It will only survive the winters in the southern part of the state, or in a well-protected spot in central New Hampshire.

Mountain Laurel (*Kalmia latifolia*)

The flowers of mountain laurel are very delicate, like petite china cups with intricate pink and white patterns. Related to rhododendrons, mountain laurel is a broadleaf evergreen plant which thrives in acidic, moist but well-drained soils. Plants in shade are open and airy; plants in sun are rounded and more dense. The leaves are bronze upon first emergence, then become glossy and dark green.

Redvein Enkianthus (*Enkianthus campanulatus*)

This shrub provides excellent scarlet-red fall color, on a par with burning bush (*Euonymus alatus*), which is no longer recommended, due to its invasive nature in some situations. When planted, the branches may be very upright, but over time the shrub will develop a beautiful horizontal branching pattern. The dainty, hanging flowers can be appreciated up close. Enkianthus requires acid, moist soils like its rhododendron relatives.

Virginia Sweetspire (*Itea virginica*)

Abundant, fragrant white flowers in summer contrast with rich green leaves, which turn shades of red and purple in the fall. Very easy to grow, this shrub thrives in sun or shade, wet or dry soils, and will sucker to form multi-stemmed colonies, which are great for a naturalized setting suitable for the warmer parts of southern New Hampshire.

Favorite Plants and Others Recommended for Woodland Areas*

Plant Name	Height x Spread	Light Requirements	Bloom Time	Bloom Color	Hardiness**	Native to NH
ANNUALS						
Baby-Blue Eyes (*Nemophila menziesii*)	4–8" x 4–8"	shade/sun	June–Sept.	blue, white		
Browallia, Bush Violet (*Browallia speciosa*)	10–24" x 12"	part shade/shade	June–Sept.	purple, blue violet, white		
Caladium (*Caladium x hortulanum*)	6"–3' x 1–3'	shade/sun	June–Sept.	n.a.		
Lobelia, Edging Lobelia (*Lobelia erinus*)	4–9" x 4 x 6"	shade/sun	June–Sept.	blue, lilac, purple, wine red, white		
Garden Impatiens (*Impatiens walleriana*)	2' x indefinite	part shade/shade	June–Sept.	all but blue		
Tuberous Begonia (*Begonia tuberhybrida*)	8–24" x 10–12"	part shade/shade	June–early Sept.	pink, peach, red orange, yellow, white, bicolors		
Wax Begonia (*Begonia semperflorens*)	6–12" x 6–12"	shade/sun	June–Sept.	pink, red, white, bicolors		
PERENNIALS						
Alkanet (*Brunnera macrophylla*)	12" x 18"	shade/part shade	April–May	blue	S	
Astilbe (*Astilbe* cultivars)	12–36" x 24"	shade/part shade	June–Sept.	red, pink, white	N,C,S	
Baltic Ivy (*Hedera helix* 'Baltica')	6" x spreading	part shade/shade	n.a.	n.a.	S	
Barrenwort (*Epimedium rubrum*)	12" x 18"	shade/part shade	May–June	pink	C,S	
Bugbane (*Cimicifuga*)	60" x 48"	sun/shade	Sept.–Oct.	white	C, S	yes
Bunchberry (*Cornus canadensis*)	4" x 12"	part shade	June–July	white	N, C, S	yes
Canadian Wild Ginger (*Asarum canadense*)	10" x spreading	part shade	n.a.	n.a.	C, S	yes
Corydalis (*Corydalis* varieties)	12" x 18"	sun/shade	May–Aug.	yellow	C, S	
Creeping Phlox (*Phlox stolonifera*)	6" x spreading	shade/part shade	May–June	purple, white	N, C, S	yes
Crested Iris (*Iris cristata*)	8" x spreading	sun/shade	May–June	purple, white	C, S	yes

Plant Name	Height x Spread	Light Requirements	Bloom Time	Bloom Color	Hardiness**	Native to NH
Dead Nettle (*Lamium* varieties)	8" x spreading	shade/part shade	June–Aug.	purple, white	C, S	
Ferns	varied	shade/part shade	n.a.	n.a.	N, C, S	some
Foam Flower (*Tiarella cordifolia*)	10" x spreading	part shade	May–June	white	N, C, S	yes
Fringed Bleeding Heart (*Dicentra eximia*)	18" x 18"	sun/shade	May–Aug.	pink, white	C, S	yes
Grapeleaf Anemone (*Anemone tomentosa* 'Robustissima')	24" x spreading	part shade	Aug.–Oct.	purple, rose	S	
Hosta, Plantain Lily (*Hosta* varieties)	varied	shade/part shade	July–Aug.	lavender, white	N, C, S	
Labrador Violet (*Viola labradorica*)	4" x 12"	sun/shade	May	violet blue	N, C, S	yes
Ligularia (*Ligularia* varieties)	36" x 48"	sun/part shade	Aug.	yellow, gold	C, S	
Lily of the Valley (*Convallaria majalis*)	6" x spreading	shade/part shade	May–June	white	C, S	
Lungwort (*Pulmonaria longifolia*)	10" x 18"	shade/part shade	April–May	purple, pink, white	C, S	
Pachysandra, Spurge (*Pachysandra terminalis*)	8", spreading	shade/part shade	May	white	C, S	
Pasque Flower (*Pulsatilla*)	10" x 18"	sun/part shade	April–May	purple	C, S	
Periwinkle (*Vinca minor*)	6" x spreading	sun/shade	April–May	lavender blue	N, C, S	
Primrose, English (*Primula denticulata*)	6" x 12"	shade/part shade	April–May	purple, white, pink	C, S	
Rodger's Flower (*Rodgersia pinnata*)	42" x 48"	shade/part shade	May–June	rose	C, S	
Sedge (*Carex morrowii*)	12" x 18"	shade/part shade	n.a.		S	
Siberian Barren Strawberry (*Waldsteinia* varieties)	6" x spreading	shade/part shade	May–June	canary yellow	C, S	
Solomon's Seal (*Polygonatum multiflorum*)	24" x 18"	shade/part shade	May–June	white	N, C, S	
Sweet Woodruff (*Galium odoratum*)	6" x spreading	shade/part shade	May–June	white	C, S	
Toad Lily (*Tricyrtis* varieties)	24" x15"	shade/part shade	Aug.–Oct.	white w/purple spots	C, S	
Yellow Foxglove (*Digitalis grandiflora*)	24" x 30"	part shade	June–July	soft yellow	N, C, S	

Plant Name	Height x Spread	Light Requirements	Bloom Time	Bloom Color	Hardiness**	Native to NH
TREES AND SHRUBS						
Carolina Rhododendron (*Rhododendron carolinianum*)	3–6' x 3–6'	part shade	May–June	white, pink, lilac	C, S	
Doublefile Viburnum (*Viburnum plicatum* var. *tomentosum*)	8–10' x 9–12'	sun/part shade	May–June	white	S	
Japanese Kerria (*Kerria japonica*)	6' x 9', spreading	sun/shade	May	yellow	C, S	
Mountain Laurel (*Kalmia latifolia*)	7–15' x 7–15'	sun/ shade	June–July	white, pink	C, S	yes
Redvein Enkianthus (*Enkianthus campanulatus*)	6–8' x 4–6'	sun/part shade	June	pink, white	C, S	
Royal Azalea (*Rhododendron schlippenbachii*)	6–8' x 6–8'	sun/part shade	May	pink	C, S	
Virginia Creeper (*Parthenocissus quinquefolia*)	climbing or spreading	sun/shade	n.a.	n.a.	N, C, S	yes
Virginia Sweetspire (*Itea virginia*)	3–5' x 3–7'	sun/shade	June–July	white	S	

*This list includes our writers' favorites and some others so is, therefore, not comprehensive.

**"N" = northern New Hampshire, "C" = central New Hampshire, and "S" = southern New Hampshire.

WOODLAND EDGES

Woodland edges are usually transition zones between sunny gardens or lawns and the more natural woodland environment. Plants that thrive in woodland edges grow under overhanging branches of larger trees and are able to tolerate an annual covering of fallen leaves.

When trees and shrubs are first planted, it's possible to grow almost anything under them. But as roots of certain trees, such as birches and maples, spread out under the soil, they can interfere with the underplantings, even if sunlight is sufficient. Under other trees and shrubs, gardeners can create lovely harmonies of plants with spring-flowering bulbs, shrubs and small trees, perennials, and annuals. Woodland-edge plants are undemanding and require little maintenance once they're established. They can endure both sun and shade, and can be combined with certain ground-cover plants to discourage weeds.

Read on to learn more about some of our writers' favorite plants for Woodland Edges. And refer to the chart that follows for details on bloom time, light requirements, and more for these plants and others our writers recommend.

Favorite Annuals for Woodland Edges
—MH

Annual Phlox (*Phlox drummondii*)
Phlox does best in a location that is at least partially shaded. Keeping the soil moist and the flowers dead-headed helps annual phlox look its best all season long. It attracts butterflies and hummingbirds (an added bonus), and will tolerate light frost. Often used to edge a bed, annual phlox is also an excellent cut flower.

Cleome, Spider Flower (*Cleome hasslerana*)
Most people either love or hate cleome, whose flowers have three or four paddle-shaped petals, a curiously stalked ovary like a hotdog on a stick, and five or six threadlike stamens. The white, pink, rose, or purple flowers create a spider-like, airy appearance. A group of them massed creates a fountain-like effect that few other annuals can equal. Cleome attracts hummingbirds and butterflies, and makes an unusual cut flower. Watch for newer cultivars that are approximately half the size of the common varieties.

Coleus (*Solenostemon scutellarioides*)
With foliage ranging in color from lime-green to red and deep purple, coleus can be used to highlight other plants or as a stunning display on its own. Provided with enough heat, coleus can fill a bare spot in four to six weeks. Grow this plant for its striking foliage, not its small, nondescript flowers.

Garden Impatiens, Busy Lizzie (*Impatiens walleriana*)
No flower brightens a shady yard like garden impatiens with its rich palette of colors. Easy to grow and covered with blooms all summer long, garden impatiens bear single or double (resembling small roses) flowers in every shade but true blue. Impatiens prefers a humus-rich, moist, but well-drained soil. If your plants go limp from drought, water them right away and they'll usually bounce back.

Nemesia (*Nemesia strumosa*)
Nemesia is an outstanding cool-season annual. Spectacular in full bloom with spurred or pouched, two-lipped flowers covering the plant, nemesia forms small mounds. Some of the newer cultivars are quite fragrant. Plan to enjoy your nemesia in spring and early summer and then, unless you live along the coast or in the north, replace it with heat-loving annuals.

Nicotiana, Flowering Tobacco (*Nicotiana x sanderae*)
Known for its clusters of narrow tubular flowers that remain open all day, nicotiana, or flowering tobacco, provides a wide range of colors. For something a little different try *N. sylvestris* (the most highly perfumed nicotiana with six-foot, candelabra-like stems of white flowers) or *N. langsdorfii* (a five-foot-tall, scentless plant with two-inch-long, chartreuse flowers).

Pansy (*Viola x wittrockiana*)
Pansies bloom heavily from the time the ground thaws until late June and again from late September into December. Flowers come in a wide range of colors. Most have centers that are bicolored or blotched with contrasting color, while others have "faces" decorated with tiny black lines like cat whiskers. What's more, pansies are edible—toss a few on a spring salad for a guaranteed conversation starter!

Pot Marigold (*Calendula officinalis*)
Pot marigolds flower all season, even tolerating light frost if planted in a partially shady location. Plants will tolerate average to poor soils as long as they are well-drained. Not only are they easy to grow, but their petals can be added to salads or rice dishes for a lovely yellow tint. Pot marigolds also attract butterflies and the flowers are ideal for cutting.

Sage, Salvia (*Salvia* species)
Gardeners treasure salvias or sages for their erect spikes (that rarely need staking) of tubular, two–lipped flowers in a wide range of colors. Most salvias are annuals in New Hampshire. If you plant salvia where it receives partial shade (especially during the hottest part of the afternoon), the sun won't bleach the flowers. Mealycup sage (*S. farinacea*) blooms non-stop until frost. Other good species are Texas sage (*S. coccinea*) and scarlet sage (*S. splendens*).

Cleome

Coleus

Foxglove

Sweet Alyssum (Lobularia maritima)
Despite all the advances in plant breeding, few plants carry all the attributes of sweet alyssum. With shearing, alyssum blooms continuously from late spring through early frost. It functions well in containers, as an edging plant, and in the border. Sweet alyssum carries a honey-sweet scent and in general outperforms many other plants. Cascading down the face of a wall or container it makes a graceful statement.

Torenia, Wishbone Flower (Torenia fournieri)
Torenia does best with shade and rich, well-drained, evenly moist soil. Plants that receive afternoon shade will have brighter flowers. Their name comes from the flower's appearance when it first opens. Wishbone flowers are a good edge or ground cover in shady beds, and look great in containers or hanging baskets.

Favorite Perennials for Woodland Edges —LvB

Big Root Geranium (Geranium macrorrhizum)
An excellent taller ground cover with fragrant foliage, big root geranium's leaves are held horizontally, thereby smothering weeds. The plant's name comes from its thickened roots, which hold water well and give it great tolerance of dry soils. Its flowers are small but pretty, and range from pale to dark pink. Big root geranium spreads by underground runners and will quickly cover a large area. An added bonus is its brilliant red fall color.

False Blue Indigo (Baptisia australis)
Baptisia is a bushy, long-lived native perennial, best planted in the back of a border or as a transition into a woodland area. Baptisia likes to stay where it's first planted. It has gray green foliage on long arching stems, lovely pea-like flowers, and dark ornamental pods, which are wonderful in dried arrangements. Baptisia tolerates a variety of soil types.

Gas Plant (Dictamnus albus)
This long-lived, shrub-like plant has glossy, lemon-scented leaves and stunning single flowers. Gas plant takes awhile to grow to maturity (it will outlive most of us) and forms a great "backbone" for any border. Its oils may cause skin irritation, so be careful handling it. Try igniting its "gas" on a calm summer evening when the flowers are in peak bloom—this will truly impress your neighbors!

Lady's Mantle (Alchemilla mollis)
This is a lovely perennial with pleated fan-like leaves that hold drops of dew in the morning. Its sprays of chartreuse flowers are understated and dry well. Try plucking them out when they've gone by, instead of cutting them back. Lady's mantle is easy to care for and reseeds readily. Plant it at woodland's edge, pondside, or on and around terraces.

Leopard's Bane (Doronicum orientale)
Leopard's bane is one of the brightest perennials of spring, with vivid yellow, daisy-like flowers rising high over bright green foliage. An excellent companion for bulbs, leopard's bane goes dormant by midsummer so plant it next to bushy plants or perennials that emerge later to cover the foliage.

Yellow Archangel

White Fringetree

Catawba Rhododendron

Peach-Leafed Bellflower (*Campanula persicifolia*)
This *Campanula*'s large bell-like flowers rise high above a short rosette of leaves (which do *not* resemble peach leaves), making this plant better for blending with other perennials than planting by itself. This bellflower reseeds itself, popping up in unexpected places but taking up so little room that it enhances its new location. Bellflower's foliage is evergreen, and its flowers are good for cutting. Pluck off spent flowers to increase bloom time.

Peony (*Paeonia* cultivars)
These old-fashioned classics are loved for their hardiness, unbelievable blooms, and handsome dark green foliage. Peonies rarely need dividing, but if you want to spread the wealth, divide them in the fall. To ensure blooms, plant eyes two inches below the surface. Double-flowered peonies can droop after a rain, so you might want to try the single or Japanese forms, which have fewer petals.

Wild Columbine (*Aquilegia canadensis*)
Our native columbine is a rugged perennial with delicate foliage and spurred flowers that seem to dance in the wind. Wild columbine prefers sandy soils with adequate moisture, but will tolerate dry soils and is less susceptible to leaf miner damage that often plagues other columbines.

Yellow Archangel (*Lamiastrum galeobdolon*)
This excellent aggressive ground cover with silver variegated leaves and soft yellow flowers will cover large areas under trees. If it becomes leggy, it will grow back very well when it is pruned. Make sure this plant has boundaries, such as dry sunny areas or water or pathways, to stop its vigorous growth.

Yellow Foxglove (*Digitalis grandiflora*)
Digitalis species are known for their tall spectacular racemes of showy flowers, resembling a cut finger of a glove (*Digitalis* means "finger-like"). Most *Digitalis* species are biennial, meaning they live for two years, but yellow foxglove lives longer than two years. Tolerant of dry soils and ideal for woodlands or woodland edges, yellow foxglove also reseeds.

Favorite Small Trees & Shrubs for Woodland Edges
—CN

Arrowwood Viburnum (*Viburnum dentatum*)
Arrowwood is a durable, dense, rounded native shrub adaptable to almost any site—even salt exposure won't faze it. Glossy green leaves contrast with blue-black berries, a favorite of birds. Cultivars ('Chicago Lustre,' 'Autumn Jazz,' 'Blue Muffin,' and 'Northern Burgundy,' to name a few) have been selected for fall color, more flowers, and fruit.

Catawba Rhododendron (*Rhododendron catawbiense*)
These large rhododendrons are spectacular in bloom but are also valuable for their big evergreen leaves. They are easy to grow, except in wet soils, but prefer acidic soils and some shade for winter protection.

Deciduous Azaleas and Rhododendrons (*Rhododendron* cultivars)

There are a number of hardy, deciduous azaleas that put on a beautiful spring show of bloom before the leaves appear. Royal azalea is one of the loveliest and most fragrant, but pinxterbloom azalea, pinkshell azalea, roseshell azalea, and 'Cornell Pink' Korean rhododendron are all excellent for central and southern parts of the state. For those who prefer brighter colors and bigger flowers, there are many hybrids from which to choose for southern New Hampshire, including the Exbury or Knap Hill hybrids, and Ghent or Mollis hybrids. The Northern Lights series of hybrids are said to be hardy to -40°F and are recommended for trial throughout the state. Be cautious when buying other azaleas—many types coming from southern or western nurseries will not survive the winter here.

Eastern Hemlock, Canadian Hemlock (*Tsuga canadensis*)

One of the few needled evergreens that tolerate shade, hemlock likes cool, moist, acidic soil which is well-drained. It also needs to be sheltered from winter winds. Hemlock makes an excellent hedge plant if pruned properly. Unfortunately, an invasive insect—the hemlock woolly adelgid—is threatening hemlocks throughout the northeast and has been found in over two dozen sites in southern New Hampshiresince 1999. The State has restricted the importation of hemlocks and hemlock products, making it difficult to find plants at nurseries and garden centers.

Kousa Dogwood (*Cornus kousa*)

A better choice for cold climates than the very popular *Cornus florida* (flowering dogwood), kousa dogwood is equally elegant but hardier with fewer disease/insect problems. It has creamy white flowers tinged with green in spring and raspberry-like (but not edible) fruit in fall. New hybrids developed at Rutgers, including 'Aurora,' 'Celestial,' 'Ruth Ellen,' and 'Stellar Pink,' are worth trying. Rather than planting it under other trees, give it its own space at the wood's edge in acidic, well-drained soil.

Large Fothergilla (*Fothergilla major*)

Shades of yellow, orange, and red blend together in the leaves of fothergilla in the fall. In the summer, dark-green foliage and pretty white bottlebrush flowers abound. Use groups of a related species, dwarf fothergilla (*F. gardenii*), in shrub beds but large fothergilla is a good choice for naturalized plantings in sun or partial shade. It prospers in acidic, moist soils, and combines nicely with azaleas and rhododendrons, which require similar conditions.

Pieris Brouwer's Beauty (*Pieris* hybrid)

Brouwer's beauty is a hybrid of two species (*P. floribunda* x *P. japonica*), more hardy than one parent and easier to grow than the other. It has shiny dark green foliage all year, purplish buds, and arching white flower panicles. Unfortunately, lacebugs can make the leaves yellow, even though it is somewhat resistant to these insects. For best performance, provide shade and acid soils, and avoid sites that expose the evergreen foliage to winter sun and wind.

White Fringetree (*Chionanthus virginicus*)

White fringetree has a graceful, silky texture when in bloom, followed by blue fruits that attract birds in the fall. It prefers moist, fertile, acidic soil, but is highly adaptable to many site conditions and shade levels. It's native to stream banks and swamp borders from New Jersey on south, but surprisingly hardy. White fringetree often has an open, spreading, shrub-like form, making a great plant for a naturalized environment along the woodland edge.

Witchhazel (*Hamamelis* species)

Witchhazels tend to grow as large, suckering shrubs along the wood's edge, but single plants can be pruned to make striking tree forms. Common witchhazel has yellow thread-like flowers in late fall; vernal witchhazel blooms in late winter/very early spring, when the bloom can be better appreciated. The petals roll up to protect themselves on very cold days, then open up again when warmer. The hybrid witchhazels ('Diane,' 'Arnold Promise,' and 'Ruby Glow') have the most impressive flowers but are limited to southern New Hampshire for hardiness.

Favorite Plants and Others Recommended for Woodland Edges*

Plant Name	Height x Spread	Light Requirements	Bloom Time	Bloom Color	Hardiness**	Native to NH
ANNUALS						
Annual Phlox (Phlox drummondii)	4–18" x 6–10"	part shade/sun	June–Sept.	white, pink, red, yellow, lavender		
Black-Eyed Susan Vine (Thunbergia alata)	4–10' vine	part shade/sun	June–Sept.	orange, yellow, white		
Cleome, Spider Flower (Cleome hasslerana)	5' x 2'	part shade/sun	July–Sept.	white, pink, purple		
Coleus (Solenostemon scutellarioides)	8–36" x 8–36"	shade/sun	June–Sept.	n.a.		
Garden Impatiens, Busy Lizzie (Impatiens walleriana)	2' x indefinite	shade/sun	June–Sept.	all but blue		
Nemesia (Nemesia strumosa)	7–12" x 4–6"	part shade/sun	May–Sept.	red, pink, yellow, lavender, purple, white		
Nicotiana, Flowering Tobacco (Nicotiana x sanderae)	2–5' x 10–24"	part shade/sun	June–Sept.	pink, red, white, chartreuse		
Pansy (Viola x wittrockiana)	6–8" x 9–12"	part shade/sun	spring and fall	purple, red, yellow, orange blue, pink, white		
Pot Marigold (Calendula officinalis)	12–30" x 12–18"	part shade/sun	June–Oct.	yellow, orange, copper, red		
Salvia (Salvia species)	1–3' x 1–2'	part shade/sun	June–Sept.	purple, scarlet, pink, white, blue		
Sweet Alyssum (Lobularia maritima)	2–12" x 8–12"	part shade/sun	May–Sept.	lavender, pink, white		
Torenia, Wishbone Flower (Torenia fournieri)	6–12" x 6–9"	shade/part shade	June–Sept.	purple, lavender and white, violet and white, pink and white bicolors		
PERENNIALS						
Alkanet (Brunnera macrophylla)	12" x 18"	part shade/shade	April–May	clear blue	S	
Autumn Joy Sedum (Sedum spectabile)	24" x 24"	sun/part shade	Sept.–Oct.	pink-bronze	N, C, S	
Avens (Geum coccineum)	12" x 15"	sun/part shade	May–July	scarlet orange	C, S	
Big Root Geranium (Geranium macrorrhizum)	15" x 24"	sun/part shade	May–June	pink	N, C, S	

Plant Name	Height x Spread	Light Requirements	Bloom Time	Bloom Color	Hardiness**	Native to NH
Black-Eyed Susan *(Rudbeckia fulgida)*	30" x 24"	sun/part shade	July–Sept.	golden yellow	N,C,S	
Cushion Spurge *(Euphorbia epithimoides)*	15" x 30"	sun	May–June	bright chartreuse	C, S	
Daylily *(Hemerocallis cultivars)*	varied	sun/part shade	June–Aug.	varies	N, C, S	
False Blue Indigo *(Baptisia australis)*	30" x 36"	sun/part shade	June–July	violet blue	N, C, S	yes
Fringed Bleeding Heart *(Dicentra eximia)*	18" x 18"	sun/shade	May–July	pink/white	N, C, S	yes
Gas Plant *(Dictamnus albus)*	30" x 36"	sun/part shade	June–July	mauve/white	N, C, S	
Great Solomon's Seal *(Polygonatum commutatum)*	70" x 24"	part shade/shade	May	white	C, S	yes
Lady's Mantle *(Alchemilla mollis)*	12" x 24"	sun/part shade	June–July	chartreuse	N, C	
Lavender Mist Meadow-Rue *(Thalictrum rochebrunianum)*	60" x 24"	sun/part shade	July–Aug.	pale purple	C, S	
Lenten Rose *(Helleborus orientalis)*	15" x 24"	part shade/shade	March–May	pink, purple, white	C, S	
Leopard's Bane *(Doronicum orientale)*	12" x 12"	sun/part shade	May–June	bright yellow	C, S	
Ornamental Grasses	varied	sun/part shade	Fall	tawny & red shades	S	
Peach-Leafed Bellflower *(Campanula persicifolia)*	30" x 18"	sun/shade	June–July	blue or white	C, S	
Peony *(Paeonia cultivars)*	36" x 36"	sun/part shade	May–June	pink, white, coral, rose	N, C, S	
Wild Columbine *(Aquilegia canadensis)*	24" x 18"	sun/part shade	May–June	red, yellow	N, C, S	yes
Yellow Archangel *(Lamiastrum galeobdolon)*	12" x 36"	shade/part shade	April–May	pale yellow	C, S	
Yellow Foxglove *(Digitalis grandiflora)*	24" x 24"	part shade	June–July	soft yellow	C, S	

SMALL TREES & SHRUBS

Plant Name	Height x Spread	Light Requirements	Bloom Time	Bloom Color	Hardiness**	Native to NH
Arrowwood Viburnum *(Viburnum dentatum)*	8–12' x 8–12'	sun/part shade	June	white	N, C, S	yes
Catawba Rhododendron *(Rhododendron catawbiense)*	6–10' x 5–8'	part shade	May–June	lavender, pink, white, red	C, S	
Common Witchhazel *(Hamamelis virginiana)*	15–20' x 15–20'	sun/part shade	Oct.–Nov.	yellow	N, C, S	yes

Plant Name	Height x Spread	Light Requirements	Bloom Time	Bloom Color	Hardiness**	Native to NH
Corneliancherry Dogwood (*Cornus mas*)	25' x 20'	sun/part shade	April	yellow	C, S	
'Cornell Pink' Korean Rhododendron (*Rhododendron mucronulatum*)	4–8' x 4–8'	sun/part shade	May	pink	C, S	
Eastern Hemlock, Canadian Hemlock (*Tsuga canadensis*)	40–70' x 25–35'	sun/shade	n.a.	n.a.	N, C, S	yes
Kousa Dogwood (*Cornus kousa*)	20–25' x 20–25'	sun/part shade	June	white/pink	S	
Large Fothergilla (*Fothergilla major*)	6–10' x 6–10'	sun/part shade	May	white	C, S	
Lowbush Blueberry (*Vaccinium angustifolium*)	6–12" x 1–2'	sun/part shade	May–June	white	N, C, S	yes
Mountain Laurel (*Kalmia latifolia*)	7–15' x 7–15'	sun/ shade	June–July	white, pink	C, S	yes
Oakleaf Hydrangea (*Hydrangea quercifolia*)	4–6' x 4–6'	sun/part shade	June–July	white	S	
Pieris Brouwer's Beauty (*Pieris* hybrid)	4–6' x 4–6'	sun/part shade	March–May	white	C, S	
Pinkshell Azalea (*Rhododendron vaseyi*)	5–10' x 5–10'	sun/part shade	May	rose pink	C, S	
Pinxterbloom Azalea (*Rhododendron periclymenoides*)	4–6' x 4–6'	sun/part shade	April–May	white, pink, violet	C, S	
Red Chokeberry (*Aronia arbutifolia*)	6–10' x 3–5'	sun/part shade	May	white	C, S	yes
Rhododendron 'P.J.M.' and other hybrids (*Rhododendron* hybrids)	3–6' x 3–6'	sun/part shade	April–May	lavender, pink	C, S	
Roseshell Azalea (*Rhododendron prinophyllum*)	2–8' x 2–8'	sun/part shade	May	pink	N, C, S	yes
Royal Azalea (*Rhododendron schlippenbachii*)	6–8' x 6–8'	sun/part shade	May	pink	C,S	
Serviceberry, Shadbush (*Amelanchier* species)	15–25' x 15–20'	sun/part shade	May	white/pink	N, C, S	yes
Smooth Hydrangea (*Hydrangea arborescens*)	3–5' x 3–5'	sun/part shade	June–July	white	N, C, S	
Summersweet Clethra (*Clethra alnifolia*)	6' x 4' (variable)	sun/shade	July–Aug.	white, pink	C, S	yes
Sweetfern (*Comptonia peregrina*)	2–3' x 2–4'	sun/part shade	n.a.	n.a.	N, C, S	yes

Plant Name	Height x Spread	Light Requirements	Bloom Time	Bloom Color	Hardiness**	Native to NH
Virginia Creeper (*Parthenocissus quinquefolia*)	climbing or spreading	sun/shade	n.a.	n.a.	N, C, S	yes
White Fringetree (*Chionanthus virginicus*)	12–20' x 12–20'	sun/part shade	June	white	C, S	
Vernal Witchhazel (*Hamamelis vernalis*)	6–10' x 8–10'	sun/part shade	March	yellow, red	C, S	

*This list includes our writers' favorites and some others so is, therefore, not comprehensive.

**"N" = northern New Hampshire, "C" = central New Hampshire, and "S" = southern New Hampshire.

Bonin

OPEN, SUNNY AREAS

These areas are free from shade and are typically taken up by lawn. Some parts, particularly slopes, may be planted with ground covers or shrubbery. However, sunny areas can also include specimen trees, plant groupings, wildflowers, and spring-flowering bulbs. Soil conditions and moisture levels of sunny areas are variable, and these locations are subject to wind and being trodden upon by pets, people, and wild animals.

Read on to learn more about some of our writers' favorite plants for Open, Sunny Areas. And refer to the chart that follows for details on bloom time, light requirements, and more for these plants and others our writers recommend.

Sunflower

Petunia, 'Supertunia'

Globe Thistle

Favorite Annuals for Open, Sunny Areas
—MH

Ageratum, Flossflower *(Ageratum houstonianum)*
Ageratum, or flossflower, has traditionally been used as an edging for the front of the border. Newer, taller cultivars have begun to appear, increasing the ways in which ageratum can be used. These new cultivars have stronger stems, making for excellent cut flowers. The blooms of ageratum last and last (the name "ageratum" means "long lived"), but cutting off flower clusters when they first turn brown will stimulate new blooms—especially important for white and pink varieties. Ageratum attracts butterflies.

Amaranthus, Love-Lies-Bleeding *(Amaranthus caudatus)*
Amaranthus, or love-lies-bleeding, bears exotic, blood-red flower clusters up to two feet in length. These tall plants with their green, purple, or red stems and light green leaves make an outstanding vertical accent in the garden. The young leaves can be eaten as a salad green and the seeds can be ground into a nutritious flour. Amaranthus is very tolerant of heat and drought, and performs best in full sun.

Annual Rose Mallow *(Lavatera trimestris)*
Rose mallow produces a profusion of cupped, hibiscus-like flowers two-to-three-inches wide on a self-supporting shrub. The botanical name, *trimestris,* means "three months" and the plants nearly bloom themselves to death during the three months they flower (right up until frost). This is one plant that dislikes overly rich soil conditions; an average garden soil is best. *Lavatera* is an excellent cut flower—be sure to cut stems with lots of buds as individual flowers last only a day or two.

Bachelor's Buttons, Cornflower *(Centaurea cyanus)*
Cornflowers are easy to grow, very frost tolerant, and given to generous self-sowing. It's simplest to sow seeds outdoors in spring when the ground is still cool. With a bit of open ground, an average soil, and some bright sun, they'll be up and growing in no time. Cornflowers have extra floral nectaries that release a 75-percent sugar solution. This solution attracts beneficial insects including lady beetles, lacewings, and flower flies.

Cosmos *(Cosmos bipinnatus)*
The daisy-like flowers of cosmos hover above a cloud of finely cut, soft fern-like foliage. Choose a planting site with full sun and poor to average, well-drained soil for best results. If plants are spaced closely (12 inches apart) staking can be avoided. Deadheading helps lengthen the bloom season. Cosmos comes in several heights and makes a good filler for the middle or back of beds and borders. Their long stems make cosmos an excellent cut flower.

Mexican Sunflower *(Tithonia rotundifolia)*
As an accent at five-to-seven-feet tall, Mexican sunflower is not easily surpassed, except perhaps by the mammoth sunflower or by castor beans. Shorter varieties are also available. The neon-orange, dahlia-like flowers have a yellow-disc center. They attract hummingbirds, moths, bumblebees, and butterflies (especially monarchs), and their bright-orange color

Ornamental Grass, *Calamagrostis*

Mugo Pine

Flowering Crabapple, 'Donald Wyman'

combines well with dark-green foliage and yellow, orange-red, and blue flowers. Mexican sunflower thrives in a hot, dry garden and deadheading keeps the flowers coming until frost.

Petunias *(Petunia x hybrida)*

It would be difficult to find another annual as versatile and dependable as this one. Petunias come in a wider range of colors than almost any other flower, are not particular about soil, and bloom through the first light frost. Petunias can be separated into two broad groups: grandifloras and multifloras. Grandifloras bear large, four-inch flowers that are best for protected spots. Multiflora petunias are bushier plants that have smaller, but more abundant flowers. Popular multifloras include the Wave, Celebrity and Carpet series. 'Supertunia' and 'Surfinia' petunias are very vigorous and bloom continuously without much care, although periodic fertilization improves performance. Petunias make excellent container plants, and also work well in beds and borders.

Snapdragon *(Antirrhinum majus)*

Snapdragons have a nostalgic appeal. Who can look at one without remembering a childhood moment of pinching open the two-lipped flower and then watching it snap shut? Snapdragons fall into three categories: dwarf (six to eight inches tall), intermediate (18 to 22 inches), and large (36 inches). They make great cut flowers and work well in massed displays or in beds and borders. Snapdragons are easy to grow and have a long bloom season (especially in cool summers). Deadheading stimulates re-bloom.

Summer Snapdragon *(Angelonia* species*)*

Summer snapdragon is a newer annual that has great potential. It grows spikes of small, orchid-like flowers on erect stems. Leaves are narrow and pointed, and are lightly scented like Concord grapes. Flowers are lavender, purple, white, or pink. This heat- and drought-tolerant annual needs warm weather to thrive, so don't plant it outside too early. Summer snapdragon is also great for beds and borders or large containers.

Sunflower *(Helianthus annus)*

No longer a tall stem topped with a simple yellow flower, sunflowers now come in a dramatic range of heights, colors, and flower sizes. Flowers can be dark red, pale to golden yellow, creamy white, or some combination. Plants are often multi-stemmed, bearing 20 or more blooms. They make excellent cut flowers, lasting up to three weeks in a vase. Sunflowers can be used in a mass planting, hedge, meadow garden, border, or container planting.

Zinnia *(Zinnia elegans)*

Few flowers are as easy to grow as zinnias. All they demand is well-drained soil, hot weather, and sun. Zinnia flowers range in size from one to four inches across and they come in a bewildering variety of forms, from a single neat row of petals to pompoms. There are zinnias for border edges, walkways, containers, and the back of the border. Pinching back the plants after they produce their third set of leaves promotes bushier, more compact growth and increases the number of flowers. Zinnias make outstanding cut flowers. Watch for varieties resistant to powdery mildew, a potential problem unless plants have extremely good air circulation.

Favorite Perennials for Open, Sunny Areas —LvB

Black-Eyed Susan *(Rudbeckia fulgida* 'Goldsturm'*)*
Black-eyed Susan, the 1999 Perennial Plant Association "Plant of the Year," is a low-maintenance yet high-impact plant for massing or specimen. It is long-blooming with large daisy-like flowers and great seed heads (the centers after the petals drop). Black-eyed Susan is one of the best and easiest perennials, and its golden yellow color can be beautiful, especially when combined with a blue or purple flowering plant.

Blue Star *(Amsonia tabernaemontana)*
Blue star is a wonderful, willowy native with the stature and size of a shrub. It has very unusual, delicate steel-blue flowers in the spring on stems that arch outward like a vase. The foliage makes a dazzling, soft-textured display that turns bright yellow in autumn. In full sun, this plant needs no support or pruning and is one of our best native perennials.

Bolton's Aster *(Boltonia asteroides)*
Bolton's aster resembles a large white aster, except that it stands up better and doesn't get mildew the way asters often do. It becomes a large clump but doesn't need staking unless planted in too much shade. Boltonia is one of the stars of the autumn garden, as it is literally covered with flowers in late September and October. 'Snowbank' is an apt name for this cultivar.

Butterfly Weed *(Asclepias tuberosa)*
Butterfly weed is certainly not a weed, but a lovely western native wildflower, with showy yarrow-like, tangerine-colored flowers and attractive seed pods. *Asclepias* is like caviar to butterflies. It is drought resistant and long-lived with quite a taproot, which is a long single root like a carrot—try not to move it once it's established. Butterfly weed is late to emerge in the spring so it's a good idea to mark its spot. With good drainage, it's a very rugged plant.

Culver's Root *(Veronicastrum virginicum)*
This native perennial resembles a veronica, with elegant white spires and deep-green leaves. You can use it as a specimen plant (its whorled foliage is interesting), or for the back of your border. Very vertical and erect, its stiff seed-head spikes provide winter interest. Culver's root is best in full sun, and some of the new varieties in pastel shades are worth checking out.

Globe Thistle *(Echinops ritro)*
The unusual spiny globes of this perennial are a wonderful contrast to the many daisy and spike flowers in the sunny meadow garden. The flowers last for weeks in the garden, but can also be dried (best done when the flowers are just opened). The grayish thistle-like foliage of *Echinops* is a great architectural and contrasting element in the garden. Globe thistle does well in poor dry soil and reseeds prolifically, but the seedlings are easy to pull if you don't want them.

Mountain Bluet *(Centaurea montana)*
A vigorous, bushy perennial with spidery, reddish-centered blue flowers appearing a few at a time, mountain bluet does best in somewhat dry conditions. Cut back mountain bluet after it blooms so it continues looking neat. It competes well in a meadow wildflower situation but looks best with other perennials, because its form is not particularly pretty alone.

Ornamental Catmint *(Nepeta sibirica/faassenii)*
The ornamental catmints are herbs with long-blooming, lavender-blue flower spikes. The shorter varieties resemble a vigorous English lavender. The leaves are scalloped and gray-green helping them to blend well in any garden. *Nepeta* can be used as informal edging plants. All ornamental catmints need good drainage, do best in full sun, and should be cut back after bloom for a flush of fresh foliage.

Ornamental Grasses
Though late to emerge in the spring, ornamental grasses create a striking vertical accent in the summer garden. Their flowers grace the fall garden and in winter, they give more interest than almost any other plant. There are many to choose from in our climate—among my favorites are *Calamagrostis* (feather

reed grass), *Miscanthus* (maiden grass), *Helictotrichon* (blue oat grass), *Panicum* (switch grass) and *Deschampsia* (tussock grass). These do best in full sun, with minimal fertilizer and maintenance. They need only to be cut back in spring.

Queen of the Prairie (*Filipendula rubra* 'Venusta')
This native meadow plant is very large and impressive, a tall, bushy plant with large, fluffy flower plumes resembling cotton candy. It withstands wind without staking and does well in boggy sites as well as in ordinary garden conditions. Queen of the prairie is aptly named and is a classic accent plant for a larger garden.

Russian Sage (*Perovskia atriplicifolia*)
I love this ornamental herb, with waving tall stems of soft gray foliage that give an airy texture and combines with nearly everything. Its blue flowers also complement other colors well. Russian sage must have good drainage and full sun to perform well. The foliage does have a distinctive sage odor when crushed, as well as a long bloom time. Russian sage was the 1995 Perennial Plant Association "Plant of the Year."

Sundial Lupine (*Lupinus perennis*)
The multi-colored, pea-like spikes of lupines are dramatic, showy, and dignified. The crisp, palmate foliage is handsome even without the flowers, yet whole festivals are arranged around lupines in bloom and it's easy to see why. This native lupine seems to be a better choice than many of the cultivars today, which are often susceptible to a fungus. Sundial lupine has crisp dark foliage, rich lavender flowers, does best in dry soil, and needs good drainage. It does tend to go dormant in midsummer, so make sure you place it with this in mind. This is the only food plant for the Karner blue butterfly, New Hampshire's state butterfly.

Yarrow (*Achillea* varieties)
Yarrows are staples of the perennial border, with gray-green lacy foliage and long lasting umbels of vivid blooms, also easily dried or cut for a fresh bouquet. They are very drought resistant, although best in moist soil. It is best to divide them every three years for continued vigor. There are many good cultivars available, including 'Moonshine,' 'Coronation Gold,' 'Summerwine,' and the 'Galaxy' hybrids.

**Favorite Small Trees & Shrubs for Open, Sunny Areas
—CN**

Note: There are literally hundreds of trees and shrubs that do well in full-sun areas, either as specimen plants or incorporated into groupings or landscape beds. In my listing of favorites, I've omitted large shade trees due to space limitations of this publication and of increasingly smaller residential landscapes. Large native trees, such as sugar maple, oak, beech, balsam fir, and white pine, are invaluable in giving us that "sense of place" that is New England, and a large landscape will almost always be enhanced by their addition.

For smaller, sunny and exposed landscape areas, the following trees and shrubs will provide limited shade, serve as focal points when installed as specimen plants, and provide structure and contrast in a plant grouping that may include perennials and annuals as well. Some are showy in bloom, and many have great fall color or winter interest. Several are good for naturalizing on slopes for erosion control.

Chinese Juniper (*Juniperus chinensis*)
Junipers are commendable for their tolerance of drought, cold, heat and poor soils as long as they get lots of sun and good drainage. Cultivars of Chinese juniper, diverse in size and growth habit, are suitable for foundation plantings, screens, accent plants, borders, ground covers, or rock gardens. It has sharp needle-like foliage, an informal spreading type of growth, and is resistant to juniper blight. Gold varieties tend to suffer winter burn. Choose varieties for desired needle color (green to blue-green to gold), shape and size, ranging from two-to-10 feet for shrub forms.

Corneliancherry Dogwood (*Cornus mas*)
This is a durable, dependable small tree or multi-stemmed shrub, often sending up suckers. It likes moist, acidic, soils but tolerates less than ideal condi-

tions. Its small flowers are bright yellow and appear very early in spring (long before the leaves)—a bright and cheery sight when you are beginning to think that winter will never end. 'Golden Glory' is a cultivar selected for abundant flowers and its summertime, cherry-like fruit is attractive to birds.

Flowering Crabapple (*Malus* hybrids)
Crabapples in bloom are truly impressive, but once the flowers are gone the foliage can become infested with disease unless resistant cultivars are used. Numerous disease-resistant varieties are available with superior flowers and attractive fruit, such as 'Donald Wyman' (white flowers), 'Prairifire' (dark pink flowers) and 'Sugartyme' (pink/white flowers). The small, red or yellow fruits persist into winter.

Japanese Tree Lilac (*Syringa reticulata*)
Its large, creamy white flower clusters appear a few weeks later than the common lilac, but unfortunately they do not have a lilac-like fragrance. It also has shiny reddish-brown bark for winter interest, and can be trained into a tree form or left to grow as a large shrub.

Japanese Stewartia (*Stewartia pseudocamellia*)
A first-class, underused ornamental with excellent flowers, form, color and bark, Japanese stewartia has large, cup-shaped white flowers with orange stamens. A fine point for winter interest is its attractive exfoliating bark, which only becomes apparent as the tree matures. This tree may be slow growing unless provided with rich, moist soils.

Lilac (*Syringa* species)
Lilac, New Hampshire's state flower, is very popular for its old-fashioned, fragrant flowers in variations of blue, lavender, pink, and white. There are hundreds of cultivars available, so making a choice depends on color preference, size, time of bloom, and resistance to powdery mildew. Many common lilacs tend to become large, unkempt shrubs. 'Miss Kim,' 'Tinkerbelle,' and 'Palabin' dwarf Korean lilac are related species, all of which are smaller (five-to-six feet) with rounded forms, making them excellent choices for a border or foundation planting.

Mugo Pine, Swiss Mountain Pine (*Pinus mugo*)
Mugo pine is an attractive, mounded evergreen shrub suitable for mass groupings or as a stand alone, low-maintenance, and not subject to attack by the common pine insect pests. Size is highly variable as varieties are often confused. The "candles," or new spring growth before the needles elongate, can be clipped in half to keep plants small. Mugo pine is suitable for growing in large containers as well, although its root ball will need winter protection.

Northern Bayberry (*Myrica pensylvanica*)
Bayberry is a tough plant for tough sites, such as open slopes and dry soils. Use it in groups for the best effect. When bruised, its leathery leaves give off a pleasant odor. Female plants produce gray waxy berries (used in bayberry candles) only if male plants are nearby, but it's impossible to tell males from females when not in bloom or bearing fruit. Late to drop their leaves, northern bayberry is also very late to leaf out in spring.

Panicle Hydrangea (*Hydrangea paniculata*)
Panicle hydrangeas bear large white panicles of old-fashioned flowers that dry nicely, and are the most dependable hydrangeas for cold climates. They provide showy, white-pink flowers in late summer when not much else is in bloom. Big-leafed hydrangea (*H. macrophylla*), the one everyone admires for its pink and blue flowers, is a gamble because of winter dieback and/or failure to bloom. It also does best in afternoon shade. Many cultivars of panicle hydrangea are available including 'Limelight,' 'Unique,' 'Compacta,' 'Praecox,' 'Kyushu,' 'Tardiva,' and 'Pink Diamond.'

Russian Arborvitae (*Microbiota decussata*)
A tough but soft-looking, low-spreading evergreen, Russian arborvitae is bright green in summer and turns bronze or purplish in the winter. It will grow horizontally about a foot a year. It makes a good spreading juniper substitute, as it has no common disease or insect problems, does best in afternoon shade, and is very cold hardy. Just make sure the soil is well-drained.

Sumac (*Rhus* species)

Long considered almost a weed, sumacs are gaining popularity as landscape plants that provide some of the brightest fall color in New England. It grows in very tough spots, but can be hard to get rid of once you've got it. I advise planting it only in natural areas where it can spread to form thickets. Its positive attributes include deep-green leaves and red conical panicles of fruit. 'Laciniata' smooth sumac was selected for brilliant fall color and cut-leaf foliage. 'Gro-Low' fragrant sumac is a superb, drought-tolerant ground cover for sun or partial shade.

Favorite Plants and Others Recommended for Open, Sunny Areas*

Plant Name	Height x Spread	Light Requirements	Bloom Time	Bloom Color	Hardiness**	Native to NH
ANNUALS						
Ageratum, Flossflower (*Ageratum houstonianum*)	4–30" x 6–12"	sun/part shade	June–Sept.	lavender-blue, lilac, white, pink		
Amaranthus, Love-Lies-Bleeding (*Amaranthus caudatus*)	3–5' x 18–30"	sun/part shade	July–Sept.	red		
Annual Larkspur (*Consolida ajacis*)	1–4' x 9–12"	sun/part shade	June–Sept.	blue, pink, purple, red, white		
Annual Rose Mallow (*Lavatera trimestris*)	2–4' x 2–4'	sun/part shade	July–Sept.	white, pink, rose		
Bachelor's Buttons, Cornflower (*Centaurea cyanus*)	8–32" x 6–8"	sun	June–Sept.	blue, pink, white, yellow		
Cosmos (*Cosmos bipinnatus*)	1–5' x 1–2'	sun	June–Sept.	pink, maroon, crimson, white		
Mexican Sunflower (*Tithonia rotundifolia*)	2–7' x 1–3'	sun	July–Sept.	orange, yellow		
Painted Tongue (*Salpiglossis sinuata*)	18–36" x 1'	sun/part shade	July–Sept.	pink, purple, red, orange, gold		
Petunias (*Petunia x hybrida*)	2' x 2'	sun/part shade	May–Sept.	pink, red, yellow, white, purple, bicolors		
Snapdragon (*Antirrhinum majus*)	8–36" x 6–12"	sun/part shade	July–Oct.	white, yellow, orange, pink, red, purple, blends		
Summer Snapdragon (*Angelonia* species)	1–2' x 12–18"	sun/part shade	June–Sept.	purple, blue, white, pink, bicolors		
Sunflower (*Helianthus annus*)	10"–15" x 1–3'	sun	July–Sept.	yellow, orange, red, purple, bicolors		
Tall Vervain (*Verbena bonariensis*)	4–5' x 16–24"	sun/part shade	July–Sept.	purple		
Zinnia (*Zinnia elegans*)	4–48" x 10–24"	sun	July–Sept.	all but blue		
PERENNIALS						
Bearded Tongue (*Penstemon* 'Husker Red')	30" x 30"	sun/part shade	July–Aug.	white	C, S	
Black-Eyed Susan (*Rudbeckia fulgida*)	20" x 32"	sun/part shade	July–Sept.	yellow	N, C, S	
Blue Star (*Amsonia tabernaemontana*)	36" x 36"	sun/part shade	June–July	soft steel blue	C, S	yes

Plant Name	Height x Spread	Light Requirements	Bloom Time	Bloom Color	Hardiness**	Native to NH
Bolton's Aster (*Boltonia asteroides*)	48" x 40"	sun	Oct.	white/pink	C, S	yes
Butterfly Weed (*Asclepias tuberosa*)	30" x 24"	sun	July–Aug.	tangerine	C, S	yes
Clustered Bellflower (*Campanula glomerata*)	30" x 18"	sun	June–July	purple	N, C, S	yes
Culver's Root (*Veronicastrum virginicum*)	60" x 30"	sun	July–Aug.	white/lavender	N, C, S	yes
Daylily (*Hemerocallis*)	varied	sun/part shade	June–Aug.	varied	N, C, S	
Evening Primrose (*Oenothera* varieties)	30" x 24"	sun/part shade	July–Aug.	yellow	C, S	
Gayfeather (*Liatris spicata*)	30" x 18"	sun/part shade	July–Aug	white or purple	N, C, S	yes
Globe Thistle (*Echinops ritro*)	36" x 24"	sun	July–Sept.	steel blue	N, C, S	
Helen's Flower (*Helenium* varieties)	48" x 30"	sun/part shade	Aug–Sept.	yellow or red	N, C, S	yes
Mountain Bluet (*Centaurea* varieties)	20" x 24"	sun	June–July	violet blue	C, S	
Mullein (*Verbascum* varieties)	varied	sun	July	pink, apricot	S	
Ornamental Catmint (*Nepeta faassenii*)	15" x spreading	sun	June–Aug.	lavender blue	C, S	
Ornamental Grasses	varied	sun	Fall	tawny or reddish	C, S	
Purple Coneflower (*Echinacea purpurea*)	24" x 30"	sun/part shade	July–Sept.	rose	N, C, S	yes
Queen of the Prairie (*Filipendula rubra*)	60" x 40"	sun/part shade	July–Aug.	soft pink	N, C, S	
Russian Sage (*Perovskia atriplicifolia*)	40" x 30"	sun	July–Oct.	light purple	C, S	
Sage (*Salvia nemerosa*)	18" x 18"	sun	June–Sept.	violet or pink	C, S	
Sea Holly (*Eryngium* varieties)	30" x 18"	sun	July–Sept.	dark violet	C, S	
Sea Lavender (*Limonium* varieties)	24" x 18"	sun	July–Sept.	soft lavender	N, C, S	
Shasta Daisy (*Leucanthemum* varieties)	varied	sun/part shade	June–July	white/yellow centers	C, S	
Sundial Lupine (*Lupinus perennis*)	24" x 24"	sun/part shade	May–June	purple	C, S	yes

Plant Name	Height x Spread	Light Requirements	Bloom Time	Bloom Color	Hardiness**	Native to NH
Sunflower (*Helianthus* varieties)	60" x spreading	sun	Aug.–Oct.	yellow	C, S	
Threadleaf Coreopsis (*Coreopsis verticillata* 'Moonbeam')	20" x 24"	sun	July–Aug.	soft yellow	C, S	
Yarrow (*Achillea* varieties)	varied	sun	June–Sept.	yellow, pink	N, C, S	yes

SMALL TREES & SHRUBS

Plant Name	Height x Spread	Light Requirements	Bloom Time	Bloom Color	Hardiness**	Native to NH
American Cranberrybush Viburnum (*Viburnum trilobum*)	8–12' x 8–12'	sun/part shade	May–June	white	N, C, S	yes
Amur Maple (*Acer ginnala*)	15–18' x 15–18'	sun	May	white	N, C, S	
Arborvitae, White Cedar (*Thuja occidentalis*)	20–30' or less	sun	n.a.	n.a.	N, C, S	yes
Beautybush (*Kolkwitzia amabilis*)	6–10' x 6–9'	sun	June	pink	C, S	
Chinese Juniper (*Juniperus chinensis*)	varies	sun	n.a.	n.a.	C, S, some N	yes
Colorado Blue Spruce, dwarf forms (*Picea pungens* 'Fat Albert,' 'Montgomery,' 'Glauca globosa')	varies	sun	n.a.	n.a.	N, C, S	
Common Ninebark (*Physocarpus opulifolius*)	5–10' x 6–10'	sun/part shade	June	white	N, C, S	yes
Corneliancherry Dogwood (*Cornus mas*)	25' x 20'	sun/part shade	April	yellow	C, S	
Fragrant Sumac 'Gro-Low' (*Rhus aromatica*)	2' x 6'	sun/part shade	April	yellow	N, C, S	
Flowering Crabapple (*Malus* hybrids)	15–25' x 10–30'	sun	May	white, pink, red	C, S	
Japanese Tree Lilac (*Syringa reticulata*)	20–30' x 20–30'	sun	June	white	C, S	
Japanese Stewartia (*Stewartia pseudocamellia*)	20–30' x 20–30'	sun/part shade	July	white	S	
Lilac (*Syringa* species)	4–15' x 6–12'	sun	May–June	blue, purple, pink, white	N, C, S	
Lowbush Blueberry (*Vaccinium angustifolium*)	6–12' x 1–2'	sun/part shade	May–June	white	N, C, S	yes
Mockorange (*Philadelphus* hybrids)	10' x 10'	sun/light shade	June	white	C, S	

Plant Name	Height x Spread	Light Requirements	Bloom Time	Bloom Color	Hardiness**	Native to NH
Mugo Pine, Swiss Mountain Pine (*Pinus mugo*)	8' x 12', variable	sun	n.a.	n.a.	N, C, S	
Northern Bayberry (*Myrica pensylvanica*)	5–10' x 5–10'	sun/part shade	May–June	inconspicuous	N, C, S	yes
Panicle Hydrangea (*Hydrangea paniculata*)	10–20' x 10–20'	sun/part shade	July–Aug.	pinkish white	N, C, S	
Rocky Mountain Juniper (*Juniperus scopulorum*)	varies	sun	n.a.	n.a.	N, C, S	
Russian Arborvitae (*Microbiota decussata*)	1' x 6'	sun/part shade	n.a.	n.a.	N, C, S	
Savin Juniper (*Juniperus sabina*)	1–3' x 4–6'	sun	n.a.	n.a.	N, C, S	
Saltspray Rose (*Rosa rugosa*)	3–5' x 5'	sun	June–Aug.	white	N, C, S	yes
Shrubby Cinquefoil (*Potentilla fruticosa*)	1–4' x 2–4'	sun/part shade	June–Aug.	yellow, white, pink, red	N, C, S	
Smokebush (*Cotinus coggygria*)	10–15' x 10–15'	sun	July–Aug	pink	C, S	
Smoothe Sumac (*Rhus glabra*)	10' x 15' or more	sun/part shade	June–July	greenish	N, C, S	yes
Wayfaringtree Viburnum (*Viburnum lantana*)	10–15' x 10–15'	sun/part shade	May–June	white	N, C, S	

*This list includes our writers' favorites and some others so is, therefore, not comprehensive.

**"N" = northern New Hampshire, "C" = central New Hampshire, and "S" = southern New Hampshire.

ROCK GARDENS

Rock gardens can be created on ledges, on sloped areas, in a formal bed near a house, or by incorporating an out-of-the-way wall or a terrace into the overall garden design. Most rock-garden plants depend on rocks or gravel to modify the environment. Some have roots that thrive in the cool, damp conditions found under stones, while others relish the heat generated by rocks basking in the sun. Some plants flourish on a stone surface while others do best growing in tiny crevices, free of competition from other plants. Many alpine species like being planted in the cool, bright shade of dwarf shrubs and all must be able to tolerate winter cold and wind.

Read on to learn more about some of our writers' favorite plants for Rock Gardens. And refer to the chart that follows for details on bloom time, light requirements, and more for these plants and others our writers recommend.

Favorite Annuals for Rock Gardens
—*MH*

California Poppy *(Eschscholzia californica)*
Gardeners who grow California poppies once are likely to grow them again, not only because they're such a satisfactory plant but also because they tend to self-seed, reappearing in the same spot the next year. California poppies have finely-divided, fern-like leaves and cup-shaped, poppy-like flowers. Providing full sun and poor-to-average, well-drained soil will yield abundant flowers. They are easiest to grow from seed because they react poorly to transplanting. Deadheading keeps the flowers coming. California poppies do well in massed plantings, on slopes, in meadows and mixed borders, and in containers.

Creeping Zinnia *(Sanvitalia procumbens)*
Traditionally easier to grow from seed, creeping zinnias make both an excellent edging and container plant. They prefer a fertile, humus-rich soil but will grow in poor, rocky, or sandy soils. The yellow, daisy-like flowers grow on low mounds of foliage with leaves resembling those of zinnia.

Dianthus, China Pink *(Dianthus barbatus x chinensis)*
The name "China pink" refers to the fringes of the petals, which look as if they have been trimmed with pinking shears. Whether planted in masses, in a rock crevice, in a border or container, dianthus's intense colors are spectacular. These plants have definite growing requirements, but once they're satisfied they're very easy to grow. Soil should be slightly alkaline (sprinkle some powdered limestone or wood ashes into the soil when planting). Dianthus also hate hot weather, so try to provide some afternoon shade. Because they're cold tolerant, dianthus can be planted outside a few weeks before the last frost date.

Gazania, Treasure Flower *(Gazania species)*
Plant gazanias in your hottest, driest, windiest spot and they'll love it! The glorious, daisy-like flowers come in yellow, oranges, pinks, bronzes, reds and whites. Petals often have a contrasting color running down the center and most have a blotch of contrasting color where the ray florets meet the pollen-bearing centers. Most flowers close during cloudy or rainy weather and at night, so be sure to locate plants for maximum sunlight. Gazanias can be massed as a ground cover, used in borders and as edging for beds, or planted in containers.

Marguerite, Boston Daisy *(Argyranthemum hybrids)*
Actually, a tender evergreen shrub, the Boston daisy bears single, semi-double or double daisy-like flowers in white, pink, or yellow on finely cut, blue-green foliage. A site in full sun with well-drained, moderately fertile soil is ideal. Used in beds and borders, Boston daisies become bushier when pinched, while deadheading encourages fuller, prolonged bloom. Boston daisies mix effectively with deep blue, purple, or other dark-colored annuals.

Marigold *(Tagetes species)*
A snap to grow from either seed or six packs of plants, marigolds fill many needs in the garden. Often used to edge a border or as a temporary hedge, marigolds also work well interplanted with other annuals in a border or container. They fall into three basic types. African marigolds (offspring of *Tagetes erecta*) carry imposing double blossoms on husky plants with flowers in gold, orange, yellow, and occasionally white. French marigolds *(Tagetes patula)* are more petite but flower more heavily, with flowers in a wider range of colors and plants that branch without pinching. Signet marigolds *(Tagetes tenufolia)* have attractive, fern-like foliage and a fresh, citrus odor. All are quite drought tolerant and actually do better in soil that is on the poor side.

Melampodium, Blackfoot Daisy *(Melampodium paludosum)*
Adapted to unpromising sites, this self-branching plant produces so many stems that it is literally covered in yellow flowers by summer's end. It's also self-cleaning, shedding its spent blossoms so there is no need to deadhead. The one thing Blackfoot daisies require is heat, so don't plant them out until the soil has warmed to at least 60° F. They look stupendous as

Scaevola, Fan Flower

Gazania

Portulaca

single plants in a rock garden or container, and very handsome when massed or used along the edge of a border.

Portulaca, Moss Rose (*Portulaca grandiflora*)

Portulaca is grown for its showy, satiny, single or double flowers. These tough plants thrive in full sun and poor, well-drained soils. The succulent leaves and stems form a coarse mat. They store moisture, allowing moss rose to flourish where most other plants can't grow. Flowers come in an array of bright colors, including hot pink, red, orange, purple, yellow and white. Like gazanias, portulaca flowers only open in sunny weather. They look terrific growing in rock crevices, along the edge of a gravel path, or in containers and hanging baskets.

Scaevola, Fan Flower (*Scaevola aemula*)

The blooms of fan flowers are unusual and appealing, and the plant thrives with little care. This plant will shine in any location that supports a sun-loving annual. As a ground cover, scaevola forms a dense carpet several feet wide. It also works well in beds and borders, and looks stupendous in hanging baskets and containers. Scaevola is happiest in a moist, well-drained soil that is high in organic matter, although it will tolerate most soils.

Strawflower (*Bracteantha bracteata*)

The strawflower is the best known everlasting of all. You can scarcely find a dried arrangement without it. Although very drought tolerant, strawflowers stay healthier and bloom better if you can keep the soil slightly moist. The papery blooms come in a wide range of colors and cut flowers last about two weeks. To dry them, harvest when the flowers are just about to open and hang them upside down in bunches for a few weeks.

Favorite Perennials for Rock Gardens —LvB

Basket of Gold (*Aurinia* varieties)

Basket of gold, a semi-evergreen, is one of the brightest perennials in the spring garden. It has a cascading form, which looks wonderful coming off of walls, in raised beds, or around rocks. Its foliage is gray-green and the cheery yellow flowers literally obscure the foliage in early spring. Plant this with spring bulbs for a stunning effect. It needs excellent drainage, and will live longer if cut back by one-third after bloom.

Bellflower, low types (*Campanula* varieties)

There are hundreds of bellflowers available, but the low types like *Campanula poscharskyana* and *Campanula carpatica* are wonderful in rock gardens. They tolerate sandy soils and dry situations, and bloom well in sun or shade. They will also have some flowers after their normal bloom time, when they're covered with white or blue bell flowers. The foliage is small and tight, and the plants stay very neat. These are great little plants.

Blue Fescue (*Festuca* varieties)

This small grass forms a compact clump, perfect for rock gardens as a specimen plant. It has very narrow blades that form a soft texture and a steely blue color that blends with practically anything. Try it with a short ground cover like thyme or mazus as an

Pinks, 'Tiny Rubies'

Stonecrop

Bearberry

TOWER HILL BOTANIC GARDEN, BOYLSTON, MA

underplanting. For a larger "fountain-type grass," try blue oat grass (*Helictotrichon*) or fountain grass (*Pennisetum*).

Hens and Chicks (*Sempervivum* varieties)
This is a classic crevice plant, with curious fleshy rosettes that send off tiny rosettes on every side as they spread. Adaptable and hardy, hens and chicks will grow in crevices, walls, and anywhere that has good drainage. The thick-stemmed flowers are coarse, but curious, and rise high above the leaves. Use hens and chicks for edging, in pots, in rock gardens, and for accenting landscape features.

Moss Phlox (*Phlox subulata*)
This classic spring-blooming ground cover commonly seen on bankings around New Hampshire in the spring is extremely durable and grows well in almost any situation, even hot dry areas. Moss phlox looks wonderful planted around rocks but spreads vigorously, so don't plant it near small, delicate rock garden plants. You can find it in a variety of colors such as purple, pink, and white.

Pinks (*Dianthus gratianopolitanus*)
The pinks are one of the few perennials with fragrant flowers and this one is perfect for rock gardens because it stays low and mounding. You can find many cultivars, such as 'Tiny Rubies' and 'Bath's Pink,' that have gray-green foliage and larger flowers than the straight species. Pinks are one of the old-fashioned perennials that once graced the gardens of our grandmothers.

Rock Cress (*Arabis sturii*)
Any of the rock cresses would work well in a rock garden. I love *Arabis sturii* (a dwarf rock cress) because its foliage is so low, and tight and glossy. It looks like a true Alpine plant and is evergreen as well. With tiny white flowers in the spring, rock cress looks fresh for the whole season. You could interplant it with other low ground covers or small rock garden plants—rock cress grows quite slowly but is worth the wait. Other *Arabis* varieties work well in rock gardens as well, such as *Arabis caucasica* (wall rock cress).

Stonecrop, low types (*Sedum* varieties)
There are so many wonderful *Sedums* to choose from and they all work well in a rock garden. Stonecrops have fleshy leaves that hold water well, so they do very well in dry areas. They come in a variety of leaf colors, such as purple, white and green, and even pink. The clustered star-like flowers look almost like dried flowers and appear in shades of pink or yellow in the late summer. Try making a tapestry of some of your favorite colors. They are extremely hardy, surviving even in the most northern parts of our state.

Thyme (*Thymus* varieties)
We could all use a little more thyme. A bad joke, I know, but true when speaking of plants. Thyme is one of the most adaptable and versatile ground covers in the perennial world. It can take foot traffic, grows quickly but not invasively, stays low, and gives a "been-there-for-a-long-time" look to any garden. In fact, some people use thyme as a lawn substitute. The only thing that bothers thyme is sitting in wet soil or too much rain, although it will bounce back. Its flowers stay low and are either purple, white or pink.

Favorite Small Trees & Shrubs for Rock Gardens
—CN

Bearberry, Kinnikinick (*Arctostaphylus uva-ursi*)
This low-growing, mat-forming ground cover has glossy evergreen leaves, dainty flowers in spring, and bright red berries in late summer. It can be difficult to transplant, so buy container-grown plants. Once established it is unusually tough and thrives on neglect, growing happily in poor, acidic, non-fertile soils. Bearberry is also very salt-tolerant.

Dwarf Fir (*Abies* species)
There are many dwarf firs that make excellent specimen plants in a rock garden. They are propagated in many cases by grafting from large trees. To name just a few for the rock garden: 'Nana' or 'Hudsonia' dwarf balsam fir, 'Compacta' white fir, 'Silberlocke' Korean fir, and 'Green Globe' Alpine fir.

Japanese Garden Juniper (*Juniperus procumbens*)
These low-growing junipers have a mounded, layered growth pattern and are excellent for rock gardens or bonsai culture. 'Nana' is the smallest cultivar, less than a foot high but spreading up to four feet.

Rockspray Cotoneaster (*Cotoneaster horizontalis*)
Rockspray cotoneaster's small, glossy green leaves change to red-orange in fall then drop; its red berries persist into winter. The horizontal branching pattern looks great spilling over slopes and rocks. 'Little Gem' and 'Tom Thumb' are particularly suitable for rock gardens because of their dwarf nature. In cold areas, a layer of loose leaves, salt marsh hay, or pine needles applied in late fall will help them overwinter safely in case there's no protective snow layer.

Favorite Plants and Others Recommended for Rock Gardens*

Plant Name	Height x Spread	Light Requirements	Bloom Time	Bloom Color	Hardiness**	Native to NH
ANNUALS						
California Poppy (*Eschscholzia californica*)	12" x 12"	sun	June–Sept.	orange, yellow, cream, red, pink		
Creeping Zinnia (*Sanvitalia procumbens*)	6–8" x 12–20"	sun/part shade	June–Sept.	yellow, orange		
Dianthus, China Pink (*Dianthus barbatus x chinensis*)	18–30" x 8–14"	sun/part shade	May–Sept.	pink, purple, red, white, bicolors		
Gazania, Treasure Flower (*Gazania* species)	6–10" x 8–10"	sun	June to Sept.	pink, red, orange, yellow, white		
Globe Amaranth (*Gomphrena globosa*)	6–12" x 6–12"	sun	July–Sept.	lilac, pink, purple, red, white		
Marguerite, Boston Daisy (*Argyanthemum* hybrids)	18–48" x 18–36"	sun/part shade	June–Sept.	pink, yellow, white		
Marigold (*Tagetes* species)	6–48" x 8–18"	sun/part shade	June–Sept.	yellow, orange, gold, red, white		
Melampodium, Blackfoot Daisy (*Melampodium paludosum*)	8–12" x 8–18"	sun	July–Sept.	yellow		
Portulaca, Moss Rose (*Portulaca grandiflora*)	4–8" x 6–18"	sun	June–Sept.	pink, red, orange, yellow, white		
Scaevola, Fan Flower (*Scaevola aemula*)	4–8" x 2–5'	sun/part shade	June–Sept.	blue, pink, purple, white		
Strawflower (*Bracteantha bracteata*)	1–5" x 8–18"	sun	July–Sept.	pink, purple, red, yellow, white		
Wall Baby's Breath (*Gypsophila muralis*)	6–12" x 1'	sun/part shade	June–Sept.	pink, white		
PERENNIALS						
Baby's Breath (*Gypsophila* varieties)	6" x spreading	sun	May–June	pale pink, white	S	
Basket of Gold (*Aurinia* varieties)	12" x 18"	sun	April–May	yellow	C, S	
Bellflower, low types (*Campanula* varieties)	4" x 24"	sun/part shade	June–July	violet blue, white	C, S	
Bitterroot (*Lewisia* varieties)	12" x 12"	sun/part shade	May–June	pink, white, salmon	S	

Plant Name	Height x Spread	Light Requirements	Bloom Time	Bloom Color	Hardiness**	Native to NH
Blue Fescue (*Festuca* varieties)	10" x 12"	sun	July	tawny	C, S	
Cinquefoil (*Potentilla* varieties)	8" x 12"	sun/part shade	June–July	white, yellow, pink	C, S	
Coral Bells (*Heuchera* varieties)	12" x 18"	sun/part shade	June–July	white, pink, red	N, C, S	
Hens and Chicks (*Sempervivum* varieties)	6" x 12"	sun	June–July	white	N, C, S	
Heron's Bill (*Erodium chrysantha*)	6" x 12"	sun	July–Aug	yellow	C, S	
Mazus (*Mazus reptans*)	2" x spreading	sun/part shade	May	purple, white	C, S	
Moss Phlox (*Phlox subulata*)	4" x spreading	sun/part shade	May–June	pink, purple, white	N, C, S	
Pinks (*Dianthus gratianaopolitanus*)	12" x 24"	sun	June–July	pink, white, crimson	N, C, S	
Rock Cress (*Arabis sturii*)	4" x spreading	sun/part shade	May	white	C, S	
Saxifrage (*Saxifraga* varieties)	6" x 12"	part shade	May	violet purple	C, S	
Snow-in-Summer (*Cerastium* varieties)	6" x spreading	sun	June–July	white	N, C, S	
Soapwort (*Saponaria* varieties)	6" x 18"	sun	June–Aug.	pink	C, S	
Stonecrop, low types (*Sedum* varieties)	6" x spreading	sun	late summer	pink, yellow	N, C, S	
Thyme (*Thymus* varieties)	2" x spreading	sun	June–Aug.	purple, white, pink	N, C, S	
Wormwood (*Artemisia* varieties)	varies	sun	n.a.	n.a.	N, C, S	

SMALL TREES & SHRUBS

Plant Name	Height x Spread	Light Requirements	Bloom Time	Bloom Color	Hardiness**	Native to NH
American Cranberry (*Vaccinium macrocarpon*)	2–6", spreading	sun	not showy	n.a.	N, C, S	yes
Bearberry, Kinnikinick (*Arctostaphylus uva-ursi*)	6–12" x 2–4'	sun/part shade	April–May	white	N, C, S	yes
Black Crowberry (*Empetrum nigrum*)	1' x spreading	sun	spring	white	N, C, S	yes
Creeping Juniper (*Juniperus horizontalis*)	1–2' x 4–8'	sun	n.a.	n.a.	N, C, S	yes
Dwarf Fir (*Abies* species)	varies	sun	n.a.	n.a.	C, S, some N	some

Plant Name	Height x Spread	Light Requirements	Bloom Time	Bloom Color	Hardiness*	Native to NH
Dwarf Spruce (*Picea* species)	varies	sun	n.a.	n.a.	N, C, S	some
Japanese Garden Juniper (*Juniperus procumbens*)	1–2' x 4–6'	sun	n.a.	n.a.	C, S	
Mugo Pine, Swiss Mountain Pine (*Pinus mugo var.* mugo)	8' x 12', varies	sun	n.a.	n.a.	N, C, S	
Rockspray Cotoneaster (*Cotoneaster horizontalis*)	12–18" x 3–7'	sun	May–June	pink	C, S	
Scotch Heather (*Calluna vulgaris*)	4–24" x 24"	sun	July–Sept.	pink	C, S	
Spring Heath (*Erica carnea*)	6–10" x 20"	sun	Jan.–March	white to red	S	

*This list includes our writers' favorites and some others so is, therefore, not comprehensive.

**"N" = northern New Hampshire, "C" = central New Hampshire, and "S" = southern New Hampshire.

WATER'S EDGES AND MARSHES

Choosing plants for these areas depends upon whether a gardener wants to emphasize form or function, and whether the body of water is a constructed pond with a dry perimeter or a natural area where water collects and flows. If visual interest is the priority, then tall, moisture-loving plants can make a dramatic statement. If the observation and feeding of pond or marsh inhabitants is the goal, then lower-growing, more naturalized plants are better suited. Woody plants or perennials along a pond or stream must tolerate wet feet, either consistently (as in a marsh) or from periodic flooding (more typical of a stream bank). Depending on the weather, these plants could also be subject to dry extremes.

Read on to learn more about some of our writers' favorite plants for Water's Edges and Marshes. And refer to the chart that follows for details on bloom time, light requirements, and more for these plants and others our writers recommend.

Favorite Annuals for Water's Edges and Marshes
—MH

Common Garden Canna (*Canna x generalis*)
Cannas have big, bold, green, maroon or variegated leaves and flowers that come in a range of hot colors. Plants get five- to six-feet tall and need heat, sun, regular fertilization, and a moist soil to grow well. This is one plant that is hard to over-water. In a cool year, plants won't begin to flower until August, but the showy flower clusters are worth the wait. Cannas can also be spectacular as the focal point in a bed, border, or container planting.

Mimulus, Monkey Flower (*Mimulus x hybridus*)
Mimulus, or monkey flowers, resemble snapdragons with their tubular shape and five lobes. Flowers are often spotted with contrasting colors and stems carry medium-green, linear leaves. Because flowers are flashy and can be an inch in diameter, this plant almost always commands attention. Mimulus will thrive in moist soils but will not tolerate drought. They will do well on the bank of a stream or even with their roots planted in soggy muck.

Favorite Perennials for Water's Edges and Marshes
—LvB

Note: There are many good water's edge plants not commonly found at garden centers, such as watershield, pickerel weed, burreed, soft stem bulrush, and arrow arum. Look for a nursery with a water garden department for some of these plants.

Astilbe (*Astilbe* cultivars)
This long-lived perennial is considered a woodland plant, yet it needs constant moisture and often struggles under trees without enough water. Planted at the water's edge, it seems much happier, especially if it can have some mid-day shade. Astilbes have lacy, finely cut foliage that is crisp and neat and has showy spires of pink, red, or white flowers in late summer.

There are many different cultivars to choose from and some, like astilbe 'Pumila,' can be used as a ground cover.

Cardinal Flower (*Lobelia cardinalis*)
This perennial is so lovely by water's edge, with its vivid, bright-scarlet blooms that seem both cooled and reflected by the water. Cardinal flower is a native wildflower that is attractive to butterflies. It reseeds so you'll have new plants each spring.

Ferns (*Ferns*)
Ferns are one of our shade garden standards. Did you know that many shade-loving plants will do well in full sun here in New Hampshire if given constantly moist soil? Ferns are so lush and lacy by water's edge, and form a lovely frame for the pool or stream. They also will grow larger here than in woodland areas. Some of the best are royal fern (*Osmunda regalis*), ostrich fern (*Matteuccia struthiopteris*), lady fern (*Athyrium filix-femina*), and hay-scented fern (*Dennstaedtia punctiloba*).

Globeflower (*Trollius* varieties)
Globeflower has low, glossy, dark-green leaves that form a neat mound. In spring tall stems of rounded flowers rise up, looking like a cross between a buttercup and a tiny yellow rose. They do beautifully in heavy damp soil, and the flowers are wonderful to watch by water's edge, as they sway in the wind. You can find them in shades of soft yellow or orange.

Joe Pye Weed (*Eupatorium maculatum*)
Joe Pye weed is a huge native wildflower that is very happy in damp soil. If you have a large pond or river, it would be a great screen or tall specimen. Joe Pye weed has impressive, large pink flowers in late summer that resemble sedum flowers. Cultivars such as 'Gateway' are improvements on the native species, but don't compromise their wild characteristics.

Ligularia (*Ligularia* varieties)
These huge-leafed perennials are happy by water's edge, and if you buy a cultivar called 'The Rocket,' make sure you give it some afternoon shade. Ligularias make wonderful architectural accents and

Canna and Coleus

Mimulus, Monkey Flower

Marsh Marigold

can be planted as specimens or in drifts. With their bright yellow or golden mid-summer flowers, they'll beautifully cover bare spots left by dormant plants.

Marsh Marigold (*Caltha palustris*)

Our native marsh marigold grows wild in streams around New Hampshire, but it's also an easy-care perennial we can have on our own pond's edge. The leaves are rounded and glossy and stay very low, and the flowers are like bright yellow water buttercups. This perennial does go dormant by mid-summer, so set a later-emerging plant nearby to cover the bare spot. Marsh marigold will grow well even in standing water.

Primrose (*Primula japonica*)

There is nothing as pretty as a drift of candelabra primroses by a pond's edge. The flowers are arranged in separate clusters up each stem, in shades of pink, orange, and purple. The leaves are heavily textured and large, and stay very crisp if given a moist area to thrive in. Make sure your primroses are in better drained areas, as they don't like to sit in water, especially when dormant. Also try the drumstick primrose, which has one large cluster atop each stem. They are one of the brightest spring bloomers.

Rodger's Flower (*Rodgersia* varieties)

This huge perennial has leaves that resemble a horse chestnut tree; they are dark green, glossy and heavily textured, often taking on bronze tinges as the season progresses. The flowers are curious clusters of light pink or white that somewhat resemble astilbe flowers.

They love moist soils and will reach four feet across or more to make a wonderful specimen plant that almost looks like a shrub.

Siberian Iris (*Iris sibirica*)

Irises look so natural at pond side, and give a great vertical accent with their long strap-like leaves. Unfortunately, the yellow flag iris (*Iris pseudacorus*) has been placed on the invasive species list for New Hampshire, so it's not a good idea to plant it, as it can displace other native species. The Siberian irises, however, are much better behaved and do very well at water's edge. They come in a variety of colors, such as purple, yellow, blue, white, even wine color, so they can make a drift of different hues. They are graceful perennials and one of my favorite pond-side plants. Japanese irises also do well, and have very large blooms.

Turtlehead (*Chelone* varieties)

Turtlehead is named for its flowers, each of which resembles the head of a turtle viewed from up close. It has glossy dark green pointed leaves, and grows very quickly by underground runners. A very adaptable and easy perennial, turtlehead is valuable because it blooms in the fall and is pink, which is an unusual color that time of year.

Rodger's Flower

Winterberry

River Birch

Favorite Small Trees & Shrubs for Water's Edges and Marshes
—CN

American Cranberry (*Vaccinium macrocarpon*)

This is a very pretty, spreading ground cover with tiny glossy green leaves in summer that turn reddish bronze in cold weather. As an extra bonus, American cranberry bears edible red cranberries (yes, the same as those available in the grocery store!). While American cranberry requires cool, moist, acidic soils with high organic matter, it doesn't need a bog.

Inkberry (*Ilex glabra*)

Inkberry is a native evergreen with small, lustrous, dark-green leaves. It makes a great background shrub, especially where soils are moist and acidic, and spreads from suckers and therefore naturalizes well. Placement on the north or east side of a building, or in a spot sheltered by trees, is ideal for winter protection. Plants are either male or female—both are necessary for berry production, a favorite food of birds.

Pussy Willow (*Salix caprea* or *chaenomeloides*)

Pussy willows are grown for their soft fuzzy catkins in early spring. My favorite is the giant pussy willow, *Salix chaenomeloides*, whose catkins are almost the size of rabbit feet. Pussy willows should be placed inconspicuously in wet, naturalized environments since their landscape interest is strictly seasonal—however, they are good for preventing erosion along waterways. Cut pussy willows back to the ground if they become overgrown. They are often short-lived, but are easily propagated and replaced.

Red Maple (*Acer rubrum*)

Also called "swamp maple" for its natural habitat, red maple does fine on upland soils as long as it doesn't dry out. Trees grown from seeds are inconsistent in form and fall color, so choose a vegetatively propagated cultivar, such as 'Red Sunset' (a.k.a. 'Franksred') or 'October Glory.' They are good choices for bright red fall foliage and are hardy in New Hampshire except in the very coldest locations. In favorable environments, red maples can reach a height of 60 feet or more.

Red-Twigged Dogwood, Redosier Dogwood (*Cornus sericea*)

Plant these shrub dogwoods where you can best appreciate their gorgeous winter stem color. The shrub in summer is upright and too tall for the front of the border, but has decent foliage, unremarkable flowers, and bluish-white berries that birds appreciate. 'Baileyi,' 'Cardinal,' and 'Isanti' are striking cultivars in winter when their bright red stems contrast against snow. Their leaves also have nice reddish purple color in the fall. Red-stemmed 'Sibirica' and yellow-twigged 'Bud's Yellow' are good choices of a closely related species, Tatarian dogwood. 'Silver and Gold' and 'Argenteo-marginata' are grown for their green and creamy white variegated leaves in summer and yellow-green stems in winter.

River Birch (*Betula nigra*)

One of the best choices for soggy sites, this birch also performs well in other areas of the landscape. It is more tolerant of heat and other stresses than the paper birch, and resistant to bronze birch borer. The peeling bark is a very attractive winter feature, especially on multi-trunk trees. 'Heritage' is a superior selection with white, tan, and salmon shades in the bark. 'Little King' or 'Fox Valley' is a good dwarf selection (10-feet high).

Summersweet Clethra (*Clethra alnifolia*)

Butterflies, bees, and people are drawn to the spicy, sweet fragrance of clethra's bottlebrush-type flowers in late summer. The leaves are a rich glossy green, changing to yellow in fall. This versatile shrub serves many functions in the landscape. Use it in borders, foundation plantings, groupings, and naturalized areas in sun or shade, as long as soils are acidic and moist. 'Compacta' and 'Hummingbird' are compact forms with white flowers. 'Pink Spires' and 'Rosea' are larger with light pink flowers, and 'Ruby Spice' has deep-pink, non-fading flowers.

Swamp Azalea (*Rhododendron viscosum*)

This is an open growing, deciduous azalea and one of the few that tolerates wet soils. The white or very light pink flowers have a nice clove-like scent.

Winterberry (*Ilex verticillata*)

The bright red berries of this native deciduous holly color our swamps and woodlands after its shiny green leaves drop in late fall. Improved cultivars including 'Red Sprite' (the most compact), 'Cacapon,' 'Winter Red,' 'Shaver,' and 'Sparkleberry' (a hybrid) have been selected for their prolific berry production and make great landscape plants. Cut some berry-laden stems and enjoy them inside during the holiday season. Birds also love them. These hollies need male plants, such as 'Jim Dandy' or 'Southern Gentleman,' nearby for fruit set and like to be planted in moist, acidic soils.

Favorite Plants and Others Recommended for Water's Edges and Marshes*

Plant Name	Height x Spread	Light Requirements	Bloom Time	Bloom Color	Hardiness**	Native to NH
ANNUALS						
Baby-Blue Eyes (*Nemphila menziesii*)	4–8" x 4–8"	shade/sun	June–Sept.	blue, white		
Black-Eyed Susan Vine (*Thunbergia alata*)	4–10' vine	part shade/sun	June–Sept.	orange, yellow, white		
Common Garden Canna (*Canna x generalis*)	5–6' x 1–2'	sun	mid-July–Sept.	red, pink, yellow, orange		
Caladium (*Caladium x hortulanum*)	6"–3' x 1–3'	part sun/shade	June–Sept.	n.a.		
Elephant Ears (*Colocasia esculenta*)	2–5' x 2'	sun/part shade	July–Sept.	n.a.		
Heliotrope (*Heliotropium arborescens*)	10–18" x 1–2'	sun	June–Aug.	lavender, purple, rose, white		
Lobelia, Edging Lobelia (*Lobelia erinus*)	4–9" x 4–6"	shade/full sun	June–Sept.	blue, lilac, purple, wine, white		
Mimulus, Monkey Flower (*Mimulus x hybridus*)	6–36" x 6–36"	shade/sun	June–Sept.	pink, orange, burgundy, yellow, cream		
Stock (*Matthiola incana*)	8–30" x 10–12"	sun/part shade	May–Sept.	white, pink, red, purple, yellow		
Torenia, Wishbone Flower (*Torenia fournieri*)	6–12" x 6–9"	shade/part shade	June–Sept.	purple, lavender and white, violet and white, pink and white bicolors		
PERENNIALS						
Astilbe (*Astilbe* cultivars)	12–36" x 24"	sun/part shade	June–Sept.	red, pink, white	N, C, S	
Beebalm (*Monarda* cultivars)	36" x 36"	sun/part shade	July–Aug.	pink, red	C, S	
Canadian Burnet (*Sanguisorba* varieties)	60" x 48"	sun/part shade	Aug.–Oct.	white	N, C, S	yes
Cardinal Flower (*Lobelia cardinalis*)	30" x 18"	sun/part shade	Aug.–Sept.	scarlet red	N, C, S	yes
Clustered Bellflower (*Campanula glomerata*)	24" x 24"	sun	June–July	purple	N, C, S	
Creeping Jenny (*Lysimachia nummularia*)	2" x spreading	sun/part shade	June–Aug.	yellow	N, C, S	

Plant Name	Height x Spread	Light Requirements	Bloom Time	Bloom Color	Hardiness**	Native to NH
Daylily (*Hemerocallis* cultivars)	varied	sun/part shade	June–Aug.	varied	N, C, S	
Ferns (*Ferns*)	varied	shade/part shade	n.a.	n.a.	N, C, S	yes
Globeflower (*Trollius* varieties)	36" x 24"	sun/part shade	May–June	yellow, orange	N, C, S	
Helen's Flower (*Helenium* varieties)	60" x 36"	sun/part shade	Aug.–Sept.	yellow, red	N, C, S	
Hosta (*Hosta* varieties)	varied	shade/part shade	July–Aug.	lavender, white	N, C, S	
Joe Pye Weed (*Eupatorium maculatum*)	84" x 40"	sun/part shade	Aug.–Sept.	pink	C, S	yes
Ligularia (*Ligularia* varieties)	40" x 48"	sun/part shade	August	yellow, gold	C, S	
Marsh Marigold (*Caltha palustris*)	16" x 18"	sun/part shade	May	yellow	N, C, S	yes
Masterwort (*Astrantia* varieties)	24" x 18"	sun/shade	June–July	pink	C, S	
Ornamental Rhubarb (*Rheum palmatum*)	60" x 40"	sun/part shade	June–July	deep red	S	
Pigsqueak (*Bergenia* varieties)	18" x 24"	sun/shade	April–May	pink	N, C, S	
Primrose (*Primula japonica*)	20" x 16"	part shade	April–May	pink, orange, lilac	C, S	
Purple Coneflower (*Echinacea purpurea*)	28" x 30"	sun/part shade	July–Sept.	deep rose	N, C, S	yes
Queen of the Prairie (*Filipendula* varieties)	64" x 42"	sun/part shade	July–Aug.	soft pink	N, C, S	
Rodger's Flower (*Rodgersia* varieties)	48" x 48"	part shade	May–June	light pink	C,S	
Siberian Iris (*Iris sibirica*)	36" x 24"	sun/part shade	June	purple, yellow, white, pink, blue	N, C, S	
Swamp Milkweed (*Asclepias incarnata*)	48" x 36"	sun	July–Aug.	pink, white	C, S	yes
Turtlehead (*Chelone* varieties)	30" x 24"	sun/part shade	Aug.–Sept.	rose	C, S	

Plant Name	Height x Spread	Light Requirements	Bloom Time	Bloom Color	Hardiness**	Native to NH
SMALL TREES & SHRUBS						
American Cranberry *(Vaccinium macrocarpon)*	2–6" x spreading	sun	May–June	pink, white	N, C, S	yes
American Hornbeam, Ironwood *(Carpinus caroliniana)*	20–30' x 20–20'	sun/part shade	n.a.	n.a.	N, C, S	yes
Black Tupelo *(Nyssa sylvatica)*	30–50' x 20–30'	sun/part shade	n.a.	n.a.	C, S	yes
Common Witchhazel *(Hamamelis virginiana)*	15–20' x 15–20'	sun/part shade	Oct.–Nov.	yellow	N, C, S	yes
Highbush Blueberry *(Vaccinium corymbosum)*	6–12' x 8–12'	sun	May	white	N, C, S	yes
Inkberry *(Ilex glabra)*	6–8' x 8–10'	sun/part shade	June	white	C, S	yes
Nannyberry Viburnum *(Viburnum lentago)*	15–20' x 10'	sun/shade	May	white	N, C, S	yes
Purpleosier Willow *(Salix purpurea)*	8–10' x 10'	sun	n.a.	n.a.	N, C, S	
Pussy Willow *(Salix caprea or chaenomeloides)*	10–20' x 10–20'	sun/part shade	March–April	grey/white	N, C, S	yes
Red Chokeberry *(Aronia arbutifolia)*	6–10' x 3–5'	sun/part shade	May	white	C, S	yes
Red Maple *(Acer rubrum)*	40–60' x 40–50'	sun/part shade	April	reddish	N, C, S	yes
Red-Twigged Dogwood, Redosier Dogwood *(Cornus sericea)*	6–10' x 6–10'	sun/part shade	June	white	N, C, S	yes
River Birch *(Betula nigra)*	40–70' x 40–60'	sun	April	brown	N, C, S	
Summersweet Clethra *(Clethra alnifolia)*	3–8' x 3–6'	sun/shade	July-Aug.	white, pink	C, S	yes
Swamp Azalea *(Rhododendron viscosum)*	2–8' x 2–8'	part shade	June	white, light pink	N, C, S	yes
Virginia Sweetspire *(Itea virginia)*	3–5' x 3–7'	sun/shade	June–July	white	S	
White Fringetree *(Chionanthus virginicus)*	12–20' x 12–20'	sun/part shade	June	white	C, S	
Winterberry *(Ilex verticillata)*	6–10' x 6–10'	sun/part shade	n.a.	inconspicuous	N, C, S	yes

*This list includes our writers' favorites and some others so is, therefore, not comprehensive.

**"N" = northern New Hampshire, "C" = central New Hampshire, and "S" = southern New Hampshire.

WATER

Because of their limited space and high-maintenance requirements, small garden ponds require particular attention from gardeners. Many plants that thrive in water can spread quickly and take over if not kept in check. From an aesthetic point of view, a gardener should maintain the proper proportion between planted areas and those remaining open water.

While there are very few trees or shrubs that grow in water, here are some perennials that do well growing in New Hampshire ponds. These plants can actually float in water. Although there are many more varieties that are not hardy in our climate, these will survive our winters.

If you're really serious about water gardening, visit your local garden center to learn about other perennials and annuals.

Read on to learn more about some of our writer's favorite perennials for Water. And refer to the chart that follows for details on bloom time, light requirements, and more for these water-loving perennials.

Favorite Perennials for Water —LvB

Arrowhead (*Saggitarius sagittifolia*)
This Japanese form of arrowhead has arrow-shaped, aerial leaves that are quite large (10-inches long). In deep water it produces ribbon-like floating leaves up to three-feet long. In summer it produces tall stems up to three-feet tall with white flowers. A double-flowered form called 'Flore Pleno' is available.

Bladderwort (*Utricularia purpurea*)
Bladderworts are insectivorous (meaning they eat insects) and thrive in water that attracts mosquito larvae. They have thread-like or rounded leaves with traps (bladders) to catch insects. The flowers are borne on leafless stems above the water.

Canadian Pondweed (*Anacharis*, a.k.a. *Elodea canadensis*)
This aquatic perennial has brittle, branching stems that are up to 10-feet long, with dark-green flat leaves. Its floating purple-green flowers bloom in mid-summer, and the plants provide excellent cover for fish and good nutrient balance in ponds. Canadian pondweed overwinters in southern New Hampshire.

Floating Heart (*Nymphoides cordata*)
Floating hearts resemble water lilies, with heart-shaped bases that grow from thin stems. Its flowers also look like those of miniature yellow water lilies held a few inches from the surface of the water. They grow best in shallow, still water.

Favorite Perennials for Water*

Plant Name	Height x Spread	Light Requirements	Bloom Time	Bloom Color	Hardiness**	Native to NH
Arrowhead (*Saggitarius sagittifolia*)	3'/spreading	sun	summer	white	S	
Bladderwort (*Uticularia purpurea*)	spreading	sun	summer	yellow	S	
Canadian Pondweed (*Anacharis*, a.k.a. *Elodea canadensis*)	spreading	sun	summer	purplish green	S	yes
Floating Heart (*Nymphoides cordata*)	spreading	sun	summer	yellow	S	yes
Pondweed (*Potamogeton*)	spreading	sun/part shade	green		S	
Water Lily (*Nymphaea odorata*)	8" x 5'	sun/part shade	summer	white	C, S	yes
Yellow Pond Lily (*Nuphar lutea*)	6' across	sun	summer	yellow	S	

*This list only includes our writer's favorites and is, therefore, not comprehensive.

**"N" = northern New Hampshire, "C" = central New Hampshire, and "S" = southern New Hampshire.

Pondweed (*Potamogeton*)
Pondweeds have submerged leaves that quickly cover muddy pool bottoms and are wonderful oxygenators in any water garden. Their floating leaves are quite decorative and many good ones can be found with different leaf effects—some are lance-shaped and others are quite rounded. This is a useful and pretty "weed!"

Water Lily (*Nymphaea odorata*)
Water lilies are the queens of the water gardens and will spread up to six-feet across. There are two types—hardy and tropical. This hardy water lily is native to the Northeast United States and has rounded glossy leaves that reach up to one-foot across, with fragrant white flowers held about eight inches above the leaves. You can look for cultivars of *Nymphaea odorata* in yellow and other colors, but make sure that they are truly hardy.

Yellow Pond Lily (*Nuphar lutea*)
Yellow pond lily has rounded, thick, dark floating leaves and paler-green submerged leaves. In midsummer, it produces bright yellow cupped flowers that are followed by berry-like fruits. Yellow pond lilies are more robust than water lilies, thriving in deeper cooler water where they may completely cover the surface.

Bonin

Beds and Borders

While beds and borders have the highest maintenance requirements of all the habitats, they often contain the showiest plants and serve as the decorative highlights of the landscape. Many plants in this habitat require a well-prepared soil and need to be weeded, fed, and watered on a regular basis; others are simply included here for design purposes. Beds and borders may contain a mixture of herbaceous perennials, small trees, shrubs, ground covers, bulbs, and seasonal bedding plants.

Read on to learn more about some of our writers' favorite plants for Beds and Borders. And refer to the chart that follows for details on bloom time, light requirements, and more for these plants and others our writers recommend.

Favorite Annuals for Beds and Borders
—MH

Blue Daisy, Blue Marguerite *(Felicia amelloides)*
The flowers on this species' best cultivars are a true blue, so it's surprising that this plant isn't more popular. Blue daisies thrive in full sun and need very well-drained soil that remains moist. Place them near the front of beds and borders, or use them to add color to a rock garden. In a container, pair blue daisies with a yellow companion to bring out the yellow flower centers.

Brachyscome, Swan River Daisy *(Brachyscome iberidifolia)*
Brachyscome, or swan river daisy, looks spectacular with its airy mounds of soft foliage topped with innumerable small, daisy-like blooms in shades of violet-blue, pink, mauve, and white. Brachyscome is very striking along the front edges of mixed plantings and in containers. It is not terribly heat-tolerant so watch for new varieties and hybrids that are longer-lived and more heat-tolerant. Brachyscome grows best in full sun, rich and well-drained soil, and will tolerate dry conditions.

Castor Bean *(Ricinus communis)*
The queen of tall annuals is the castor bean. It can be used at the back of the border or positioned within the border to provide shade for lower growing flowers. With its bamboo-like stem and star-shaped, deeply notched leaves, this plant is an attention-grabber wherever it grows. Leaves come in shades of green, red, and dark purple. Castor bean prefers growing conditions with heat, a rich and moist soil, and full sun. On an exposed site, it may need staking. Castor bean should not be grown where children play, because all parts of the plant are poisonous if eaten.

Celosia, Cockscomb *(Celosia argentea)*
Suitable for a position just in back of the border's edge, celosias also make a fine cut flower. Celosias are divided into two very different groups. Prince's feather *(C. argentea plumosa)* produces woolly spires of flowers that are remarkably feathery. Cockscomb *(C. argentea cristata)* is actually a mutant with flowers in convoluted ridges that look like furry brains. Both varieties bloom in bright shades of red, yellow, and orange. Look for new pastel shades (less brazen) or try wheat celosia *(C. spicata)* for a slightly different look. Celosias thrive in hot, humid weather.

Dahlia *(Dahlia* hybrids*)*
There is no lack of choice when it comes to dahlias, with more than 20,000 different cultivars ranging from one-foot dwarfs for border edging to 10-foot giants for the back of the border. The showy flowers come in an array of shapes and sizes, from tiny daisy-like singles to dinner-plate-sized doubles. Give dahlias full sun and a site with rich, well-drained soil and watch them grow! Plan to stake the taller hybrids. Dahlias are also a favorite with florists because of their bright colors and long vase life.

Fountain Grass *(Pennisetum setaceum)*
For the most intense color, plant fountain grass in full sun. It will definitely be a standout, with its beautiful maroon to reddish foliage, graceful mounded profile, and delicate, arching flower spikes. Unlike most other grasses, *P. setaceum* will flower throughout the growing season, not just at the end. It can be placed near the back of the border, in the middle as a vertical accent, or be grown with other annuals in containers. Left in the garden, it creates winter interest. When cut and dried, fountain grass makes a handsome addition to dried arrangements.

Geranium *(Pelargonium* species*)*
Give geraniums full sun, water, and a rich, well-drained soil and their needs are met. Most are outstanding in bedding displays, window boxes, and containers. The key to geraniums is distinguishing the various groups.

Most common are zonal geraniums *(P. x hortorum)*. These are the geraniums you often see on windowsills. Their leaves are marked with a dark, horseshoe-shaped band (the zone). Their claim to fame is stalks of large, rounded, single or double flowers in an amazing array of colors.

Dahlia

Zonal Geranium

Threadleaf Coreopsis

Ivy geraniums *(P. peltatum)* creep and trail much like an ivy. They even have ivy-shaped leaves. They look wonderful trailing over the edge of a container or window box.

Regal or Martha Washington geraniums *(P. domesticum)* were a Victorian favorite. Their blooms resemble azaleas and they flower most prolifically in early summer while the weather is still cool.

Another group are the fragrant or scented geraniums. Most carry common names indicative of the scent carried on the leaves, such as lemon, nutmeg, coconut, apple, peppermint, and rose-scented geraniums.

A newly popular group are the fancy-leaf geraniums. Grown for their brilliantly colored leaves, the flowers are definitely secondary. Leaves may be gold, silver, tricolored, white-margined, marbled, net veined and/or deeply lobed. Fancy-leaf geraniums can stand alone or be used to highlight the colors of adjacent annuals.

New Guinea Impatiens *(Impatiens* hybrids*)*
These sturdy plants carry foliage in shades of green, bronze or variegated in combinations of green, red, bronze and yellow. They tolerate much brighter light than garden impatiens and can be placed in full sun if they get shade for just a few hours a day. Their flowers are also much more flamboyant, measuring two to three inches in diameter, and are a real-eye catcher along the edge of the border or in a container.

Nierembergia, Cup Flower *(Nierembergia caerulea)*
A favorite in Victorian times, nierembergia or cup flower is enjoying a period of renewed popularity. It forms a lovely compact, spreading mound of finely-cut foliage capped by numerous cup-shaped flowers in violet or white. Nierembergia is a ground hugger, making it perfect for the front of the border, a window box, or a spot in the rock garden. Shearing the tops after each period of heavy bloom will keep it flowering throughout the summer.

Stock *(Matthiola incana)*
Although the flowers are pretty, stock is really grown for its intense, clove-like scent. Preferring cool weather, stock will bloom most prolifically in spring and fall, fading during the heat and humidity of high summer. Their unmistakable fragrance has made stock a favorite cut flower as well as insuring its popularity in beds and borders.

Favorite Perennials for Beds and Borders —LvB

Aster *(Aster cultivars)*
These are an autumn-blooming favorite with daisy-like flowers in shades of pink and purple. Their rich colors give a depth and brightness to fall gardens that few perennials can do. Look for the tall New England asters *(Aster novae-angliae)* or the shorter New York asters *(Aster novi belgii)*. Powdery mildew can be a problem with these perennials but if you select resistant varieties, give them good drainage and put plants in front of the bottom half of the asters to hide the mildew.

Mallow

Single Mums

Forsythia 'Northern Gold'

Garden Phlox (*Phlox paniculata*)

One of the staples of the sunny border, garden phlox is tall and bright, with large clusters of showy and spectacular pink, red, or white flowers. However, garden phlox has a reputation for being highly prone to mildew. New mildew-resistant selections have recently been developed—these plants may still get mildew, but only on a small percentage of the leaf area. Otherwise, you can try thinning your clumps in spring to a few strong stems, which will give larger flowers and have less mildew. Also plant other perennials or annuals in front of your phlox to hide the mildew.

Hollyhocks (*Alcea rosea*)

Hollyhocks are easy to grow, with large saucer-shaped blossoms that are arranged around tall spikes. They bloom for a long time, and are stately at the back of a border or naturalized around foundations. Although hollyhocks are short-lived, they're also self-sowing, with young plants popping up in all kinds of unexpected places. They tend to decline after bloom, so make sure they have other plants in front of them.

Larkspur (*Delphinium* cultivars)

When one thinks of a cottage or an English garden, this is one of the first plants to come to mind. *Delphiniums* are magnificent, though short-lived, perennials with tall blue, pink, or white spires. Pacific hybrids need staking because they can reach almost seven feet but if you want a shorter *Delphinium* think about purchasing one of the *belladonna* types. Larkspurs require a lot of fertilizer, and a well-drained but

moist soil to do well. Slugs and other pests bother them, so I consider them high-maintenance perennials but worth the effort.

Mallow (*Malva alcea*)

These are somewhat similar to hollyhocks but smaller, with light-green, deeply cleft leaves and clusters of long-lasting flowers that open for many weeks. Best in full sun, mallow will take dry conditions. They are a wonderful cottage perennial for a sunny border and can be used in the middle or front sections of the border, as the flowers are airy and light textured.

Shasta Daisy (*Leucanthemum* cultivars)

Formerly known as "chrysanthemum," shasta daisies are one of the standards in the perennial world, with their familiar showy white flowers and ease of cultivation. I highly recommend a cultivar called 'Becky,' because it has lovely foliage and large vivid flowers. This one is the national Perennial of the Year for 2003 so it should be easy to find. There are also some very short (12-inch) varieties available such as 'Snow Lady.' All shasta daisies need good drainage and division every two to three years. If you remove the spent flowers, they will bloom for a longer time.

Single Mums (*Dendranthema* cultivars)

These single fall mums are truly hardy and a much superior garden plant to the double forms, which are incorrectly called "hardy mums." The graceful single daisies give valuable late-fall color, as well as a great nectar station and landing pad for migrating butterflies. Easy and vigorous, single mums can be sheared mid-season for more compactness and should be divided every three years.

Sunflower Heliopsis (*Heliopsis* varieties)
Resembling true sunflowers (*Helianthus*) but smaller, 'Summer Sun' is compact with large daisy-like flowers. These sunflowers are one of the brightest in the summer garden, and are very easy to care for.

Threadleaf Coreopsis (*Coreopsis verticillata*)
Another Perennial Plant Association Plant of the Year (1992), threadleaf coreopsis is one of the easiest and blendable perennials around. Threadleaf coreopsis is fast-growing, durable, and long-blooming with delicate airy foliage. This perennial is the perfect plant to cover the dying foliage of bulbs or plants such as large bleeding heart that goes dormant in the summer. The cultivar 'Moonbeam' has dark foliage that contrasts nicely with the pale yellow flowers.

Favorite Small Trees & Shrubs for Beds and Borders
—CN

Anglojap Yew (*Taxus* x *media*)
Yews are the predominant foundation plant in many landscapes because of their adaptability to sun or shade, moist or dry soils, and low maintenance requirements. What they can't tolerate is excessive deer browsing, a major problem in some areas. They are often sheared into strange shapes or flat-topped, but are most attractive if selectively pruned rather than sheared. Yews make good hedges, screens, and accents. There are many good cultivars including 'Brownii,' 'Densiformis,' 'Nigra,' and 'Hicksii.' 'Taunton' is much less susceptible to winter burn than others.

Blue Holly, Meserve Holly (*Ilex* x *meserveae*)
Shiny evergreen leaves and bright red berries make blue holly a winter beauty, but these plants are attractive all year round. Plant them in a sheltered location on the east or north side of your home in moist, acidic soil—they can be kept small with proper pruning. 'Blue Girl,' 'China Girl,' and 'Blue Princess' are all female clones and need a male pollinator, such as 'Blue Boy' or 'Blue Prince,' to produce the bright red berries.

Creeping Juniper (*Juniperus horizontalis*)
The low growth, feathery texture, and foliage coloration makes this plant a great filler in the shrub or perennial border or in the foundation planting. There are many popular cultivars that range from mint green ('Prince of Wales') in color to silvery green ('Hughes'), gray green ('Andorra compacta'), or blue ('Blue Prince'). Most turn purplish in cold weather. Flat-growing "rug types" include 'Wiltoni,', 'Blue Rug,' and 'Bar Harbor.' All are drought tolerant and adaptable to almost any site. Unfortunately, juniper blight can be a problem in wet weather.

Forsythia (*Forsythia* hybrids)
How would we know when spring is here if not for the bright yellow flowers that give forsythia its reason for being? Left unpruned, it can become a messy, unkempt shrub the rest of the year. Rather than planting individual bushes, combine a few low-growing forsythia with other shrubs in a border. Flower buds above the snow line are often killed by cold. 'Gold Tide' is a neat, low-growing forsythia, which also means its buds will be protected by snow cover most winters. Other varieties recommended for flower-bud hardiness include 'Sunrise,' 'New Hampshire Gold,' 'Meadowlark,' 'Northern Gold,' 'Northern Sun,' and 'Vermont Sun.' 'Lynwood Gold' has a better form and excellent flowers but may not be as hardy.

Japanese Maple (*Acer palmatum*)
This aristocratic tree needs extra winter protection as it's marginally hardy, but it's worth the effort for its elegant form, foliage color, and texture which contrasts nicely with greenery or granite. 'Bloodgood' (reddish-purple leaves) and 'Dissectum Atropurpureum' (thread-like green leaves) are the most cold hardy varieties and offer excellent spring and fall color. Put them in a well-tended, well-drained, partially shaded shrub border protected from wind and heavy snow loads, and mulch deeply with leaves for winter.

Japanese Spirea (*Spiraea* species)
There are many new cultivars of compact, pink-flowered spireas that make nice additions when grouped in the border. The old standard 'Anthony Waterer' Bumald spirea has been superceded by cultivars of Japanese spirea with many variations on foliage and flower color. 'Magic Carpet' and 'Neon Flash' have reddish or bronze spring leaf color and deep-pink flower color. 'Limemound,' 'Gold Mound,' and 'Golden Princess' have yellowish to lime-green foliage and lighter flower color. For nice fall leaf color, try 'Goldflame' or 'Norman.'

Norway Spruce, dwarf forms (*Picea abies*)
'Nidiformis' or bird's nest spruce grows slowly to three-to-six-feet high and wide, rounded in form with a depression in the top that makes a nest-like appearance in the rock garden or border. 'Pumila' is similar but more even more rounded and less susceptible to winter burn. 'Pendula' is a weeping type, variable but a good novelty plant. Be careful only to use these dwarf forms in your foundation plantings, as the regular Norway spruce is a very large tree and has no place in a small landscape.

Rhododendron 'P.J.M.' (*Rhododendron* 'P.J.M.' hybrids)
The original P.J.M. hybrid has bright lavender-pink flowers and leaves that are small, dark green in summer and reddish purple in fall and winter. Now there are many related hybrids—many bred at Weston Nurseries in Massachusetts—with variations on the flower color and equally as hardy. Ask a specialist at your garden center to help you choose one suitable for your area.

Shrub Rose (*Rosa* species)
Everyone loves the beautiful, fragrant flowers of rose; however, many roses are difficult to grow due to disease and insect problems and pruning requirements. There are many introductions of low-maintenance shrub roses for us to grow that are hardy and somewhat disease-resistant, including but certainly not limited to 'Carefree Beauty,' 'Carefree Wonder,' 'Seafoam,' and 'The Fairy.'

Star Magnolia (*Magnolia stellata*)
Star magnolia is the most cold-hardy magnolia and offers lovely, white, star-like flowers that develop from fuzzy pink buds before the leaves appear. This dense, multi-stemmed large shrub or tree grows best in a protected location, so can be integrated into a shrub border near a building. Avoid southern exposures or star magnolia may flower too early and be harmed by a freeze. 'Centennial' is relatively fast growing and dependable. Another group of magnolias to try are the Loebner hybrids, including 'Leonard Messell' with fragrant pink and white flowers.

Viburnum (*Viburnum* species)
Include a fragrant viburnum in the shrub border near a walkway for the utmost enjoyment of the large, snowball-like clusters of highly fragrant flowers in May. Koreanspice viburnum, Burkwood viburnum, and Judd viburnum are all good choices for the warmer areas of New Hampshire, but they're not as cold-hardy as some other viburnums that lack fragrance.

Favorite Plants and Others Recommended for Beds and Borders*

Plant Name	Height x Spread	Light Requirements	Bloom Time	Bloom Color	Hardiness**	Native to NH
ANNUALS						
Blue Daisy, Blue Marguerite (*Felicia amelloides*)	10–24" x 10–24"	sun	May–Sept.	blue, lavender, mauve, white		
Brachyscome, Swan River Daisy (*Brachyscome iberidifolia*)	8–18" x 12–18"	sun	May–Sept.	violet, pink, mauve, white		
Castor Bean (*Ricinus communis*)	3–9' x 2–4'	sun/part shade	July–Sept.	pink, red, yellowish-green		
Celosia, Cockscomb (*Celosia argentea*)	8–36" x 6–16"	sun/light shade	June–Sept.	pink, red, orange, yellow, cream		
Dahlia (*Dahlia* hybrids)	1–10' x 12–48"	sun/part shade	July–Sept.	most but true blue		
Dusty Miller (*Senecio cineraria*)	8–12" x 6–10"	sun/shade	May–Nov.	yellow		
Fountain Grass (*Pennisetum setaceum*)	3–5' x 18–24"	sun	July–Sept.	pinkish		
Geranium (*Pelargonium* species)	4–36" x 8–14"	sun	May–Sept.; year-round indoors	pink, red, orange, purple, white, bicolors		
New Guinea Impatiens (*Impatiens* hybrids)	8–24" x 12–18"	sun/part shade	June–Sept.	rose, red, salmon, pink, orange purple, white, bicolors		
Nierembergia, Cup Flower (*Nierembergia caerulea*)	8" x 8"	sun/part shade	May–Sept.	violet, white		
Scabiosa (*Scabiosa atropurpurea*)	18–36" x 9"	sun	June–Sept.	purple, blue, pink, white		
Stock (*Matthiola incana*)	8–30" x 10–12"	sun/part shade	May–Sept.	white, pink, red, purple, yellow		
Sweet Pea (*Lathyrus odoratus*)	6–72" x 12"	sun/part shade	May–Sept.	blue, pink, purple, red, white		
PERENNIALS						
Aster (*Aster* cultivars)	varied	sun/part shade	Sept.–Oct.	pink, purple, white	N, C, S	yes
Basket of Gold (*Aurinia saxatilis*)	12" x 18"	sun	April–May	yellow	S	
Bearded Tongue (*Penstemon* 'Husker Red')	30" x 30"	sun/part shade	July–Aug.	white	C, S	

Plant Name	Height x Spread	Light Requirements	Bloom Time	Bloom Color	Hardiness**	Native to NH
Beebalm (*Monarda* cultivars)	36" x 30"	sun/part shade	July–Aug.	purple, pink	C, S	
Checker-Mallow (*Sidalcea* varieties)	30" x 18"	sun/part shade	July–Aug.	pink	S	
Garden Phlox (*Phlox paniculata*)	32" x 36"	sun	Aug.–Sept.	pink, purple, white	N, C, S	
Helen's Flower (*Helenium* varieties)	48" x 30"	sun/part shade	Aug.–Sept.	yellow, red	N, C, S	yes
Hollyhocks (*Alcea rosea*)	60" x 24"	sun/part shade	July–Sept.	pink, red, purple, salmon, white, yellow	C, S	
Larkspur (*Delphinium* cultivars)	48–70" x 24"	sun	June–July	blue, pink, white	C, S	
Mallow (*Malva alcea*)	30" x 24"	sun/part shade	July–Sept.	pink	S	
Oriental Poppy (*Papaver orientalis*)	24" x 24"	sun	June–July	orange, pink, white	N, C, S	
Peony (*Paeonia* cultivars)	36" x 36"	sun/part shade	May–June	pink, white, coral	N, C, S	
Shasta Daisy (*Leucanthemum* varieties)	varied	sun/part shade	June–July	white/yellow centers	C, S	
Single Mums (*Dendranthema* varieties)	20" x 24"	sun	Sept.–Oct.	pink	C, S	
Sunflower (*Helianthus* varieties)	60" x 36"	sun	Aug.–Oct.	yellow	C, S	
Sunflower Heliopsis (*Heliopsis* varieties)	36" x 18"	sun/part shade	July–Oct.	yellow	C, S	
Threadleaf Tickseed (*Coreopsis verticillata*)	20" x 24"	sun	July–Aug.	soft yellow	C, S	
Wolfsbane (*Aconitum napellus*)	40" x 36"	sun/part shade	July–Aug.	dark blue	C, S	

SMALL TREES & SHRUBS

Plant Name	Height x Spread	Light Requirements	Bloom Time	Bloom Color	Hardiness**	Native to NH
Anglojap Yew (*Taxus* x *media*)	15–20' x 5–8'	sun/shade	n.a.	n.a.	C, S	
Blue Holly, Meserve Holly (*Ilex* x *meserveae*)	4–15' x 4–15'	sun/part shade	not showy	n.a.	S	
Boxwood (*Buxus microphylla* var. *koreana*)	3–4' x 3–4'	sun/part shade	not showy	n.a.	C, S	
Burkwood Viburnum (*Viburnum* x *burkwoodii*)	8–10' x 6–7'	sun/part shade	May	white	C, S	
Creeping Juniper (*Juniperus horizontalis*)	1–2' x 4–8'	sun	n.a.	n.a.	N, C, S	yes

Plant Name	Height x Spread	Light Requirements	Bloom Time	Bloom Color	Hardiness**	Native to NH
Dwarf Alberta Spruce (*Picea glauca* var. *albertiana*)	10–12' x 8–10'	sun	n.a.	n.a.	C, S	
Dwarf Fothergilla (*Fothergilla gardenii*)	2–3' x 2–3'	sun/part shade	May	white	C, S	
Dwarf Korean Lilac (*Syringa meyeri* 'Palibin')	4–6' x 6–8'	sun	May–June	purple	N, C, S	
Forsythia (*Forsythia* hybrids)	3–10' x 5–10'	sun	April–May	yellow	C, S	
Greenstem Forsythia (*Forsythia viridissima* 'Bronxensis')	2–3'	sun/part shade	April–May	yellow	C, S	
Highbush Blueberry (*Vaccinium corymbosum*)	6–12' x 8–12'	sun	May	white	N, C, S	yes
Japanese Maple (*Acer palmatum*)	6–20' x 6–25'	sun/part shade	May–June	red	S	
Japanese Spirea (*Spiraea japonica*)	2–5' x 3–5'	sun	June–Aug.	pink	N, C, S	
Judd Viburnum (*Viburnum* x *juddii*)	6–8' x 6–8'	sun/part shade	May	white	C, S	
Koreanspice Viburnum (*Viburnum carlesii*)	4–6' x 4–6'	sun/part shade	May	white	S	
Lilac 'Miss Kim' (*Syringa patula* 'Miss Kim')	4–6' x 4–6'	sun	May–June	purple	N, C, S	
Norway Spruce, dwarf forms (*Picea abies*)	4–15' x 4–12'	sun	n.a.	n.a.	N, C, S	
Rhododendron 'P.J.M.' (*Rhododendron* 'P.J.M.' hybrids)	3–6' x 3-6'	sun/part shade	April–May	lavender pink	C, S	
Rose (*Rosa* species)	varies	sun	June–Aug.	white, pink, red, yellow	C, S	
Star Magnolia (*Magnolia stellata*)	15–20' x 10–20'	sun	April–May	white	C, S	
Summersweet Clethra (*Clethra alnifolia*)	4–8' x 4–6'	sun/shade	July–Aug.	white, pink	C, S	yes
Vanhoutte Spirea (*Spirea* x *vanhouttei*)	6–8' x 10–12'	sun	May–June	white	N, C, S	
Weigela (*Weigela florida*)	6–9' x 6–9'	sun	June–July	pink to red	C, S	
Willow 'Hakuro Nishiki' (*Salix integra* 'Hakuro Nishiki')	4–6' x 4–6'	sun/part shade	n.a.	n.a.	C, S	

*This list includes our writers' favorites and some others so is, therefore, not comprehensive.

**"N" = northern New Hampshire, "C" = central New Hampshire, and "S" = southern New Hampshire.

CONTAINER PLANTINGS

Container plantings bring your garden closer to home—on your front porch, on your deck, in a window box—often in a visually striking way. There are many plants suitable for planting in containers, which can be anything from clay pots, to barrels, to old Radio Flyer wagons. One challenge with container plantings is to keep them well-irrigated as they tend to dry out faster than plants in the ground, especially those in full sun on hot days. Another challenge is that the growth of plants' roots is limited by the container's size and by the close proximity of neighboring plants in the container. Overwintering perennials and trees or shrubs in containers requires special effort, because the roots are the least hardy part of the plant and will be killed if left in an above-ground container all winter.

Read on to learn more about some of our writers' favorite plants for Container Plantings. And refer to the chart that follows for details on bloom time, light requirements, and more for these plants and others our writers recommend.

Million Bells

Petunias, Marguerite, Creeping Zinnia,
Marigolds, and Million Bells

Sweet Potato Vine (with Swedish Ivy)

Favorite Annuals for Container Plantings —MH

Bacopa, Sutera *(Sutera cordata)*

This plant's outstanding characteristic is its trailing stems that can reach two-feet long by summer's end. When cascading over the edge of a container, hanging basket, or stone wall, bacopa is very effective. It has small green leaves covered with tiny white flowers from late spring until frost. New shades have appeared on the market in recent years. Pinching the plant a few times when it is young encourages fuller growth.

Bidens, Golden Goddess *(Bidens ferulifolia)*

Bidens produces one-to-two-inch yellow, daisy-like flowers with a yellow center. There are short, medium, and tall strains as well as trailing types that look great in a container. Bidens's ferny foliage and thin stems will weave their way through other plants, pushing their yellow faces to the foreground. Try to keep the soil slightly moist; bidens will tolerate drought, but tends to flower less under drought conditions.

Common Garden Verbena *(Verbena hybrids)*

Depending on the cultivar, garden verbena can be erect and bushy or creeping. The creeping forms are lovely cascading over the lip of a container or window box. Garden verbena also serves well as an edging plant. It has four-sided stems and tubular flowers with five lobes. The flowers are held in dense clusters that cover the plant all summer long. Many of the modern hybrids are available only as vegetatively produced plants.

Common Lantana *(Lantana camara)*

Tiny, trumpet-shaped flowers are grouped into round clusters on lantana. Adding to its attractiveness, different flower colors are produced within each cluster, and often the individual flowers change color with age. Its long, trailing branches look especially fine spilling over the sides of a container. Lantanas actually prefer poor to average well-drained soils. They flourish in warm to hot weather and flower most prolifically in full sun. Be aware that lantana flowers and foliage are toxic—wear gloves when handling plants and keep them out of the reach of pets and children.

Diascia, Twinspur *(Diascia barberae)*

Diascia or twinspur, a native of South Africa, is a member of the snapdragon family. It has become extremely popular in the last few years, mainly due to its great performance in containers. It looks especially fine paired with silver foliage. Try combining it with licorice plant *(Helichrysum petiolare)*. Diascia is not particularly heat-resistant, so expect it to bloom most profusely in spring and late summer. Shearing it back by a third after one flush of bloom may help force another. The name "twinspur" refers to the two downward-pointing spurs on the small trumpet-shaped flowers.

Fuchsia *(Fuchsia hybrids)*

Fuchsias are grown for their showy, pendulous flowers in shades of pink, red, purple, and creamy white. Plants range in size from tiny to gigantic, and from upright to bushy, trailing, or hanging. They all need a rich, well-drained, moist soil. Morning sun with af-

Hosta

Pigsqueak

Ornamental Grass, *Helictotrichon*

ternoon shade is ideal. They are outstanding plants in containers and hanging baskets. Place them where you can enjoy the hummingbirds who will surely visit for nectar.

Heliotrope *(Heliotropium arborescens)*

Heliotrope is an old-fashioned annual, grown in the late 1800s for the sweetness and delicacy of its scent. Although many of the newer hybrids have little scent, the flowers, which bloom in clusters six-to-nine-inches across, are beautiful even without the scent so attractive to bees and butterflies. The leaves are deeply ribbed, dark green, and suede-like in appearance, giving them an attraction of their own. Try heliotrope in combination with lighter colors and softer textures for a striking contrast.

Licorice Plant *(Helichrysum peitiolare)*

Licorice plant is grown for its woolly or hairy, heart-shaped leaves. It is a semi-trailer, growing more outward than up, eventually arching downward under the weight of its stems. It weaves its way among other plants, enhancing their appeal so much that it is now a staple in containers. Besides the usual silver-leafed form, there are some interesting cultivars. A chartreuse leaf form is called 'Limelight' (also 'Aurea') and variegated versions carry the names 'Roundabout,' 'Variegatum,' and 'Rondello.' This plant is very vigorous and can overwhelm slowly growing annuals. A smaller-leafed variety, 'Petite Licorice,' seems to grow more slowly.

Million Bells *(Calibrachoa hybrids)*

Million bells resemble a bushy, trailing, miniature petunia. Outstanding in containers, million bells can be used almost anywhere in the garden, even as a ground cover. They are quite drought-tolerant and will flower heavily throughout the summer. Try one of the newer cultivars like 'Terra Cotta' with brick-red, to orange, to yellow, and bicolored flowers all on one plant. And be sure to keep an eye out for new hybrids with more colors and larger flowers.

Nasturtium *(Tropaeolum majus)*

Nasturtiums are easy-to-grow, mound-forming or climbing plants. They are favorites for window boxes, baskets, and containers of all types. Their leaves, buds, and flowers are edible. As cut flowers, nasturtiums have a long vase life. Most are sweetly scented and attract hummingbirds. Most people grow nasturtiums for their two-inch flowers which form wide trumpets and have a long spur at the back. The secret to growing nasturtiums is benign neglect. Plant them in poor to average soils and don't overfertilize or overwater them.

Ornamental Pepper *(Capsicum annuum)*

Unlike most annuals, ornamental peppers are grown for their fruits, not their flowers. These peppers are simply decorative cultivars of the edible pepper, almost always from the hot side of the family. Most have many small fruits that are held upright. Some peppers start out green and pass through several colors before reaching their mature shade (red, orange, yellow, purple, chocolate brown). When harvesting and slicing peppers for cooking, wear plastic gloves so you don't inadvertently burn your hands or eyes (by rubbing them). Ornamental peppers are attractive, not only in containers but also as an edging or massed display.

Osteospermum, Cape Daisy (*Osteospermum ecklonis* hybrids)

Grown for its showy, daisy-like flowers in shades of purple, yellow, white, orange, or pink, osteospermum is a great container plant. It will bloom its head off during cool spring weather, slow down during summer heat and humidity, and begin blooming heavily again in fall (if protected from frost). Providing well-drained soil and full sun (osteospermum won't open in shade or cloudy weather) insures good performance. Osteospermum is also beautiful in a rock garden.

Pentas, Star Cluster, Star Flower (*Pentas lanceolata*)

Pentas bears rounded or flat clusters of tubular flowers each with five lobes or stars. It prefers full sun and evenly moist soil, so combine it in a container with plants that won't suffer from too much water—canna, elephant's ear (*Colocasia esculenta*), or creeping Jenny (*Lysimachia nummularia*) work well. Keep an eye out for pentas hybrids which generally only reach a height of one to three feet (sometimes grouped with the compact forms of *P. lanceolata*).

Pimpernel (*Anagallis monellii*)

Pimpernel is gaining popularity as more and more gardeners discover this brilliant, deep gentian-blue container plant. In fact, pimpernel is starting to give edging lobelia a run for its money. Its small flowers, centered with a splash of rosy-red, can inspire some wonderful color combinations. Pimpernel prefers light, sandy soils so feel free to use it in the rock garden or edging a border. Also keep an eye out for scarlet pimpernel (*Anagallis arvensis*). The flowers are brick-red with a honey-like scent.

Sweet Potato Vine (*Ipomoea batatas*)

Ornamental sweet potato is an excellent plant for containers or border edges. Grown for their foliage alone, ornamental sweet potatoes fall into two basic groups: those with chartreuse, heart-shaped leaves and those with dark purple leaves that almost look black. All are easy-to-grow heat lovers. Put them in a protected spot where wind can't tear the leaves and watch them grow!

Favorite Perennials for Container Plants —LvB

Note: Most perennials will not survive the winter in pots, but you can put them in a root cellar, cut them back, water them once, and most of the time they'll come through. The advantage is that you will have larger plants than if you start each year with annuals. The following are some perennials that have nice foliage for combining with annuals in containers.

Creeping Jenny (*Lysimachia nummularia* 'Aurea')

A vigorous ground cover with small, golden coin-like leaves, and long trailing runners, creeping Jenny looks great spilling out of containers. It's also an excellent contrast to purple or dark-green foliage. Flowers are single and fragrant, but not as noticeable on 'Aurea' as on the green form.

Hosta, Plantain Lily (*Hosta* varieties)

Hosta is not only one of the great garden foliage plants but also a nice container plant, with large leaves that can be found in all sorts of colors and variegations. They can be planted as specimens or combined with trailing plants or smaller annuals for a lovely effect.

Ligularia (*Ligularia* varieties)

You need to keep this one well watered, but its huge leaves provide wonderful architectural accents and contrasts to ferny foliage in containers. You can also use ligularia plants by themselves. Look for the cultivar 'Othello' or 'Desdemona' for rounded leaves, green on top, and purple on the undersides.

Ornamental Grasses

Grasses such as blue oat grass (*Helictotrichon*) and fountain grass (*Pennisetum*) make lovely container plantings, by themselves or combined with small or trailing plants. An ornamental grass in a container on either side of a walkway makes a wonderful formal accent to an entrance.

Ornamental Rhubarb *(Rheum palmatum)*

Ornamental rhubarb has huge coarse leaves that contrast well with finer textured plants. Look for purple selections such as 'Atrosanguineum' for a stunning effect.

Periwinkle (*Vinca minor*)

A classic evergreen ground cover for shade or sun that doubles well as a container plant, periwinkle has long runners that trail over the sides of pots, leaving plenty of room for other plants in the middle. It has violet flowers in the spring, but you can find white or burgundy-flowered varieties as well.

Pigsqueak (*Bergenia cordifolia*)

Bergenia has huge, waxy evergreen leaves, which make a fine container addition, especially paired with delicate annuals. It doesn't grow too quickly to "hog the pot" and sends up pretty dark-pink flowers in the spring, before most container plants begin flowering.

Favorite Small Trees & Shrubs for Container Plantings
—CN

Note: Shrubs and small trees suitable for containers are those that grow slowly, tend to stay small, or are easily maintained by pruning. However, none of them should be expected to survive the winter in an above-ground container, since sub-freezing temperatures would kill the roots. (See the section on Caring for Your Plants, page 75, for overwintering methods for dormant plants in containers.) On the other hand, you can grow some marginally hardy plants in containers, such as bigleaf hydrangea and tree peony, if you overwinter them properly. Other small trees and shrubs recommended for containers which have been covered in previous sections of this book include:

Arborvitae, small cultivars (Thuja occidentalis)
Boxwood (Buxus microphylla)
Creeping Juniper (Juniperus horizontalis)
Dwarf Spruce (Picea *species*)
Japanese Maple (Acer palmatum)
Lilac 'Miss Kim' (Syringa patula *'Miss Kim'*)
Mugo Pine (Pinus mugo)
Rockspray Cotoneaster (Cotoneaster horizontalis)
Rose (Rosa)
Shrubby Cinquefoil (Potentilla fruticosa)
Spirea (Spiraea japonica)
Weigela (Weigela florida)

Bigleaf Hydrangea (*Hydrangea macrophylla*)

Purchase a container-grown plant in the garden center and enjoy its large blue, pink, or white globe-like or lace-cap blooms in late summer. Next year's flower buds are formed before winter, so protecting the buds from winter kill is essential for repeat bloom. In the landscape, the plants are usually killed back and do not re-bloom.

Dwarf Korean Lilac (*Syringa meyeri* 'Palibin')

One of the smallest types of lilacs, this fine-textured, tidy lilac blooms when young. It has dainty violet purple flowers in late spring and small shiny dark green leaves, resistant to powdery mildew.

Harry Lauder's Walking Stick (*Corylus avellana* 'Contorta')

A European hazelnut, this plant is grown for its twisted and curling branches, especially visible after leaves fall and in early spring. So leave it out late and get it out early to enjoy its unusual form. It grows very slowly and can easily be kept to a size suitable for a container. Use the cut branches in floral arrangements—just don't cut too many! Remove any suckers that grow from the base of the plant if it has been grafted, as they will not have the desired contorted growth.

Tree Peony (*Paeonia suffruticosa*)

Tree peony's huge, scented, silky blooms and clean green foliage on an erect, woody shrub are spectacular in a formal container. Purchase plants that are at least three-years old, as they may not bloom until age four to five, and plant them two to three inches deeper than they were in the original container. Water and fertilize consistently, store them carefully over the winter, and prune only broken stems in spring.

Willow 'Hakuro Nishiki' (*Salix integra* 'Hakuro Nishiki')
The coloration on this wispy willow makes it a standout in a container or in the shrub border. The long, slender stems are reddish pink, and the narrow green leaves spotted and streaked with pink and white. Cut it back in the winter before storing it to increase the number of stems next year.

Favorite Plants and Others Recommended for Container Plantings*

Plant Name	Height x Spread	Light Requirements	Bloom Time	Bloom Color	Hardiness**	Native to NH
ANNUALS						
Bacopa (*Sutera cordata*)	3" x 12–24"	sun/part shade	June–Sept.	white, pink, violet, red, white		
Bidens, Golden Goddess (*Bidens ferulifolia*)	12–30" x 12–18"	sun	June–Sept.	yellow		
Butterfly Flower (*Schizanthus pinnatus*)	1–4" x 9–18"	sun	June–Sept.	pink, purple, red, yellow, white		
Cigar Flower (*Cuphea ignea*)	12–24" x 12–24"	sun/part shade	June–Sept.	fiery red with black and white tip		
Common Garden Verbena (*Verbena* hybrids)	10–20" x 12–20"	sun/part shade	June–Sept.	pink, purple, salmon, red, white		
Common Lantana (*Lantana camara*)	6–72" x 1–6'	sun/part shade	June–Sept.	white, pink, yellow, red, lilac, purple		
Diascia, Twinspur (*Diascia barberae*)	6–10" x 20–24"	sun/part shade	May–Sept.	pink, salmon, rose		
Flowering Maple (*Abutilon* hybrids)	18–96" x 18–72"	sun/part shade	June–frost	white, yellow, orange, pink, red		
Fuchsia (*Fuchsia* hybrids)	6–60" x 12–42"	sun/part shade	June–Sept.	pink, purple, red, pink, white, orange		
Heliotrope (*Heliotropium arborescens*)	10–18" x 1–2'	sun	June–Aug.	lavender, purple, rose, white		
Licorice Plant (*Helichrysum petiolare*)	20" x 1–5'	sun/part shade	May–Oct.	silver, chartreuse or green		
Million Bells (*Calibrachoa* hybrids)	6–10" x 18–36"	sun/part shade	May–Sept.	pink, violet, blue, red, yellow		
Nasturtium (*Tropaeolum majus*)	8–15" x 12–18"	sun/part shade	June–Sept.	yellow, orange, cream, red, mahogany, pink		
Ornamental Pepper (*Capsicum annuum*)	8–30" x 8–15"	sun	flowers in July, fruit in Sept.	fruit is red, orange, yellow, purple, brown		
Osteospermum, Cape Daisy (*Ospeospermum ecklonis* hybrids)	1–5' x 1–4'	sun	May–Sept.	purple, yellow, white, orange, pink		
Pentas, Star Cluster, Star Flower (*Pentas lanceolata*)	1–6' x 1–3'	sun	May–Sept.	pink, magenta, purple-red, lilac, white		
Pimpernel (*Anagallis monellii*)	4–8" x 12–18"	sun/part shade	June–Sept.	deep blue, red, pink		
Sweet Potato Vine (*Ipomoea batatas*)	8" x 1–8'	sun/part shade	n.a.	chartreuse, purple		

Plant Name	Height x Spread	Light Requirements	Bloom Time	Bloom Color	Hardiness**	Native to NH
PERENNIALS						
Ajuga, Bugleweed (*Ajuga lamiaceae*)	4–6"	shade/part shade	May	blue, white	N, C, S	
Baltic Ivy (*Hedera helix*)	7" x spreading	part shade/shade		green	C, S	
Barrenwort (*Epimedium* varieties)	12" x spreading	shade/part shade	May–June	pink	C, S	
Coral Bells (*Heuchera* varieties)	12–18" x 12–24"	sun/part shade	July–Aug.	pink, white, red	C, S	
Creeping Jenny (*Lysimachia nummularia*)	2" x spreading	sun/part shade	June–Aug.	yellow	C, S	
Cushion Spurge (*Euphorbia epithymoides*)	15" x 30"	sun	May–June	chartreuse	C, S	
Dead Nettle (*Lamium* varieties)	8" x spreading	shade/part shade	June–Aug.	purple, white	C, S	
Ferns	varied	shade/part shade	n.a.	n.a.	N, C, S	yes
Hardy Geranium (*Geranium* varieties)	varied	sun/part shade	June	pink, white	C, S	
Hosta, Plantain Lily (*Hosta* varieties)	varied	shade/part shade	July–Aug.	lavender, white	N, C, S	
Lady's Mantle (*Alchemilla mollis*)	12" x 24"	sun/part shade	June–July	chartreuse-yellow	N, C, S	
Lamb's Ears (*Stachys* varieties)	10" x 18"	sun	June–July	purple	C, S	
Lenten Rose (*Helleborus* varieties)	15" x 24"	part shade/shade	March–May	pink, purple, white	C, S	
Ligularia (*Ligularia* varieties)	36" x 48"	sun/part shade	Aug.	yellow	C, S	
Ornamental Grasses	varied	sun/part shade	fall	tawny, red	S	
Ornamental Rhubarb (*Rheum* varieties)	48" x 36"	sun/part shade	June–July	deep red	C, S	
Peony (*Paeonia* cultivars)	36" x 36"	sun/part shade	May–June	pink, white	N, C, S	
Periwinkle (*Vinca minor*)	6" x spreading	sun/shade	April–May	purple, white	C, S	
Pigsqueak (*Bergenia cordifolia*)	16" x 24"	sun/shade	April–May	pink	C, S	
Plume Poppy (*Macleaya* varieties)	84" x spreading	sun/part shade	July–Aug.	bronze pink	C, S	
Rodger's Flower (*Rodgersia* varieties)	40" x 48"	shade/part shade	May–June	rose pink	C, S	
Threadleaf Coreopsis (*Coreopsis verticillata*)	20" x 24"	sun	July–Aug.	yellow, pink, red	C, S	

Plant Name	Height x Spread	Light Requirements	Bloom Time	Bloom Color	Hardiness**	Native to NH
SMALL TREES & SHRUBS						
Bigleaf Hydrangea *(Hydrangea macrophylla)*	2–5' x 2–5'	sun	July–Aug.	blue, pink, white	S	
Dwarf Korean Lilac *(Syringa meyeri* 'Palibin')	4–6' x 6–8'	sun	May	purple	N, C, S	
Harry Lauder's Walking Stick *(Corylus avellana* 'Contorta')	3–8' x 3–8'	sun/light shade	May–June	tan catkins	S	
Tree Peony *(Paeonia suffruticosa)*	2–6' x 2-6'	sun/afternoon shade	spring	pink, red, yellow, white	C,S	
Willow 'Hakuro Nishiki' *(Salix integra* 'Hakuro Nishiki')	4–6' x 4–6'	sun/part shade	n.a.	n.a.	C, S	

*This list includes our writer's favorites and some others so is, therefore, not comprehensive.

**"N" = northern New Hampshire, "C" = central New Hampshire, and "S" = southern New Hampshire.

PART II

Taking Care of Your Garden and Landscape

Bonin

Designing Your Garden and Landscape
—LvB

When you're planning the location of your garden, pay attention to your normal vantage point. Where do you spend time in relation to your garden? Do you like to sit outside? If so, where? Also, if you're away or very busy during part of the year, choose flowers that bloom when you'll be around and able to enjoy them.

Perennials and Annuals
Select perennials with a variety of bloom times to assure color most of the season. Annuals, on the other hand, bloom for much of our New Hampshire summers, but some take longer to reach blooming size.

Colors and textures are personal preferences. Cool colors, such as blues or greens, and fine textures, recede visually and calm you. Warm colors, such as reds or yellows, and bold textures, come forward and create excitement. Try to contrast fine textured foliage (smaller leaves) with plants that have large bold leaves. This creates interest and focal points in the garden. In working with color, you can create an effective unifying motif by repeating groups of a color (flower or foliage) throughout the whole garden.

Create informal effects with curves, and formal effects with geometric shapes and straight lines. Simply creating a curved edge on a border gives a more casual feeling than a straight line.

Most people put taller plants in back and shorter plants in the front. You can create depth and interest by putting some tall material in mid or frontal positions instead of in back. Also look for plants such as *Heuchera* (coral bells) that have low foliage but airy taller flowers for the front of a border.

Most designers, unless using large plants as single specimen plants, clump three to five (or more) of one variety together for a more natural looking effect. Nature creates triangles rather than squares.

Rules of thumb for spacing plants are:

1. Clump-forming plants
   a) short plants (under 20 inches) around 12–18 inches on center.
   b) mid-range plants (20–30 inches) around 24 inches on center.
   c) taller plants need 30–36 inches on center.

2. Indefinitely spreading plants (ground covers) have some guidelines, but each plant has a different growth rate, so tailor spacing to your taste and budget.

Borders should be no more than seven-feet wide to allow someone to work from either side pulling weeds or cutting flowers. Leave a pathway of about three feet next to a building if your garden is planted next to it. If your garden is wider than seven feet, create paths that meander through it so you avoid walking on the soil. Wide, flat stones can make a fine path. If your path doesn't lead through to a destination on the other side, you can create one with a small terrace, bench, or garden sculpture.

Annuals can be used well with perennials because they have a much longer season of bloom. Many designers put "pockets" of annuals throughout their gardens, as well as shrubs and small trees. This is called "the mixed border" and is considered the new American garden ideal.

Small Trees & Shrubs

Trees and shrubs are chosen primarily for their show of foliage, their architectural forms, their colored or textured bark, and their ornamental and/or edible fruit.

Make sure you know the mature height and width your new woody plants will attain. Often it takes many years to attain full size, but many people are dismayed when their foundation plants begin to cover windows and crowd the building behind them. In most cases it is difficult to keep them in scale by pruning as it ruins the shape of the shrub. Consider the shade patterns cast by trees. It is usually desirable to provide summer shade but winter sun on your home. Plant large trees at least 30 feet from the building.

When choosing trees, think how the mature shape will relate to the buildings or other trees near it. For example a tall upright building may want a more spreading tree to balance it. Specimen trees are usually planted singly, but many small trees and shrubs look best in-groups of three, five, or seven, or planted in mixed borders with perennials and annuals.

Learn whether your woody plant is evergreen (foliage that remains green all year) or deciduous (leaves or needles that are shed each fall and re-grow in the spring). You may want to put some of each in for a varied effect. Try to plant evergreen shrubs so they aren't exposed to southwestern wind and sun, as this desiccates their leaves. Remember that many woody plants have different color foliage—red, golden, variegated, etc. Check out which ones also have autumn color. (See list on page 80.)

Winters here in New Hampshire are very long. Think about finding trees with beautiful bark such as stewartia, or shrubs with colored branches for a lovely winter effect such as red-twigged dogwood. Many berries, such as those on winterberry, persist through much of the winter.

When choosing woody plants for their fruit, look for pest-resistant varieties that will require less spraying, and for hardy varieties that are proven in New Hampshire. If you're interested in having a hospitable habitat for birds and wildlife, there are many wonderful shrubs and trees that offer berries and nuts for them. Try planting a "bio-border" with a variety of these plants.

Although flowers are often a bonus, rather than a primary concern, try to plant shrubs and trees together that differ in their bloom times. A majority that you find in garden centers will bloom in the spring, but you can find many that bloom in the summer, fall, and even the winter.

Choosing the Best Plants
—*CN*

Landscape plants represent substantial investments of money and time. Planning your design and selecting what plant species to use brings you to the garden center or nursery looking for healthy, high-quality plants that will perform well in your garden or landscape. Resist the temptation to buy plants off the discount rack to save a little money. Purchasing fresh, well-cared for, and uninfested plants will pay off many times in your garden. Some general things to look for when buying plants are:

- Vigorous, healthy new growth
- Good foliage color
- Freedom from diseases and insects
- No weeds in the pots (even though they're free, you don't need them!)
- Plant size in proportion to the container or root ball
- Good plant shape and structure
- No broken stems or branches or other mechanical injury
- Well-rooted in the container but no circling or matted roots, especially on trees and shrubs
- Root tips light in color rather than dark and mushy, which indicates rot
- Well-watered plants (wilted plants indicate lack of proper care)

Annual bedding plants are usually sold in bloom. Choose young plants that aren't overgrown for the size of the pot and that have some buds but few open flowers.

Perennial plants may be purchased in containers or, in some nurseries, as field-grown plants. Bare-root plants are also common when ordering by mail. Any of these are acceptable as long as the plant is properly cared for. Make sure the roots don't dry out on fresh-dug or bare-root material, and that you plant them in the garden as soon as possible. Bare-root plants have a limited shipping season and must be planted when dormant, but they may be stored in the refrigerator for a short time. Container-grown plants can be kept in the pots as long as needed, provided they are watered regularly.

Most trees and shrubs are readily available as container-grown stock. They can be sold and planted into the landscape at any time from early spring to late fall, and are easy to handle without special equipment. If grown too long in the container, roots tend to develop in circles inside the wall of the container and the plant can become root-bound. Circling roots should be cut before transplanting, otherwise they will continue to enlarge and may eventually "girdle" or strangle the plant.

Large deciduous trees, most evergreen trees, and some large shrubs are also marketed as balled-and-burlapped (B&B) product. These plants are grown in field nurseries, then dug while dormant in early spring or late fall. The root balls are wrapped tightly in burlap and, may be placed in a wire or mesh basket. The root ball should be intact and firm, not loose or broken. Field-grown plants are very heavy due to the weight of the soil ball, and many homeowners can't handle large B&B stock. Rough handling (such as dropping the root ball from the back of a truck) will cause root breakage.

Trees and shrubs are permanent additions to the landscape and poorly shaped or structured plants only get worse as they grow. Shrubs should be full, with several stems originating from the bottom portion of the plant. Deciduous trees should be pruned in the nursery to have a single trunk, not co-dominant stems. (The following drawing on the far right shows correct pruning—the others do not.) Branches should be evenly spaced along the trunk and the foliage should be distributed throughout the top two-thirds of the tree.

Incorrectly pruned   Correctly pruned

Branch growth should be angled out well from the trunk, rather than tending towards vertical. The trunk of the tree should be free of ridges, cankers, wounds, and cracks. Small pruning wounds that are healed are acceptable. The trunk should be tapered and the root flare (base of the stem where first roots attach) visible at the top of the root ball or container. The tree should be able to support itself in an upright position without staking or tying.

Evergreen trees should have a single central leader or trunk, with branches growing nearly horizontally. In most cases, branches should extend all the way to the ground. Pruning and training should have been done in an appropriate way to preserve the natural shape of the species or cultivar.

When it comes to nursery stock, bigger isn't always better. Research has demonstrated that smaller plants are often able to become established and resume normal growth faster than larger plants of the same species (dwarf cultivars not withstanding). Compare, for example, a one-inch trunk diameter Norway spruce with a two-inch diameter Norway spruce, both planted at the same time. After a few years, the smaller plant will equal or exceed the one that was originally larger in size. This, of course, assumes that the plants are given proper care after transplanting, especially an adequate amount of water. Small plants are also better-suited for poorly drained or compacted soils, where they are able to establish roots in the top few inches of soil and avoid the underlying problem.

Of course, many people still want to purchase as large a plant as they can afford, in order to create an "instant landscape." Whatever size plant you select, the root ball should be in proper proportion to the above-ground portion. Your nursery or garden center specialist can help you choose well-proportioned trees and shrubs.

Planting Your Plants Properly
—MH

Most plants grow best in well-drained, fertile soils. In many gardens, this requires amending or altering the present soil. To determine if this is necessary, have the soil analyzed at a testing laboratory. Soil test results determine soil type, pH level (acidity or alkalinity), and the quantities of important plant nutrients. Get a soil-test kit by visiting your local UNH Cooperative Extension office (see the county-by-county listing at the end of this book) or by calling UNH Cooperative Extension's toll-free Family, Home & Garden Education Center Info Line (1-877-398-4769). Simple soil-test kits are also available at many garden centers.

When buying perennials or trees and shrubs, ask if the nursery or garden center has specific recommendations for planting. If none are available, follow the general planting tips in this section. If your plants are covered by a warranty, make sure to carefully follow the retailer's guidelines. Failure to do so may affect the warranty (when applicable) and the success of your planting.

Planting Annuals

Most annuals need full sun for at least four to six hours a day to flower well. Choose shade-tolerant species such as impatiens, coleus, or begonias for locations that receive less sun.

Good bed preparation is essential for good performance of annuals. Beds should be deeply spaded, to a depth of six to eight inches if possible. Water retention can be improved in sandy soils by mixing in two to three inches of sphagnum peat moss, leaf mold, compost, or rotted manure. If possible this should be done several weeks before planting.

Base applications of fertilizer and lime on the results of a soil test for best results. In the absence of a soil test, add a complete fertilizer such as 10-10-10 at the rate of one pound per 100 square feet of bed area or a complete slow-release fertilizer following label directions. A pH of 5.8 to 6.5 is satisfactory for most annuals. Most New Hampshire soils are acidic and require the addition of lime to correct pH. Incorporate lime and fertilizer into the top four to six inches of soil after mixing in the soil amendments. Rake the soil surface smooth.

Annuals in Containers

Many annuals grow well in a variety of containers, such as hanging baskets, window boxes, and large pots. Containers should be chosen not only for aesthetics, but should be proportional to the type and number of plants to be grown in them. The one single requirement for any container is that it has an adequate drainage hole (or holes).

Artificial soils (soilless media) are usually easy to use and give good results. A variety of ready-to-use products is available commercially. Those which have approximately 50% peat and 50% perlite work well. Watering and fertilizer requirements will differ among containers. Generally, annuals in containers will require more water and fertilizer than similar annuals grown in beds.

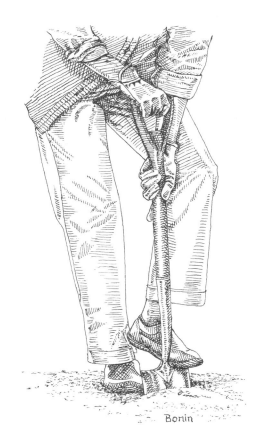

Bonin

Planting Procedure for Annuals

Wait to plant tender annuals until all danger of frost has passed. For most of New Hampshire, the last frost date is around June 1. Many annuals, even if not injured by low temperatures, won't grow well until the soil warms. Plant annuals with the top of the roots just under the surface of the soil. Be sure to remove paper, fiber, and plastic pots before planting. Remove the upper edges of peat pots so that the pot will not act as a wick, pulling water away from the roots. Pinch off any buds and flowers when planting to promote better branching and a stronger plant. Once transplanting is complete, water the plants thoroughly.

Planting Perennials

Good bed preparation is essential for good performance of perennials. Beds should be deeply spaded, to a depth of eight to 12 inches if possible. All soils can be improved by mixing in two to four inches of sphagnum peat moss, leaf mold, compost, or rotted manure. Apply dolomitic limestone at the rate of five to 10 pounds per 100 square feet for a new bed. Select a complete fertilizer, or use an organic or slow-release one. If possible, beds should be prepared in the fall before planting.

Make sure the soil is well-drained. To determine if an area is poorly drained, dig a hole about 10-inches deep and fill it with water. The next day fill the hole again and see how long the water remains in it. If it drains away in less than 10 hours, drainage is satisfactory for most perennials. In some situations, it may be necessary to install underground drainage lines or construct raised beds.

Dig a hole twice the depth of the pot. Backfill, making sure the surface of the soil in the pot is level with the surface of the garden.

As you plant, be sure to loosen the roots on the bottom of the plant. If the root ball is very dense, make a two-inch vertical cut in the bottom of the root system. Water plants thoroughly, then mulch with one-half to one inch of organic matter. Don't pack the mulch tightly around the plant base.

Planting Trees and Shrubs

Proper planting techniques for trees and shrubs is important because buying these woody ornamentals is often a big investment. That's why you need to ask your retailer for specific planting instructions.

Research has shown that improper planting depth is the major cause of plant mortality. This is especially true with balled and burlapped plants because the trunk flare and soil line are hidden beneath the burlap, making it difficult to determine the height of the root ball.

Always handle trees and shrubs by their root balls or containers and not by their tops—the heavy weight of the soil will injure root hairs. Remove plants from their containers just prior to planting, so plants will not sit on the ground in the hot sun. Water the plants three hours before planting.

Dig a hole two to three times as wide as the root ball and as deep as the height of the ball. If the plant is balled and burlapped, loosen the burlap and feel the top of the ball for an accurate measurement. When planting a tree, make sure the trunk flare remains above ground level. If planted too deep, the roots will suffer from lack of oxygen.

Planting Procedure for Trees and Shrubs

Place the plant in the planting hole with the trunk flare one inch above the surrounding soil. Place a straight stake or yardstick across the hole to help determine planting depth.

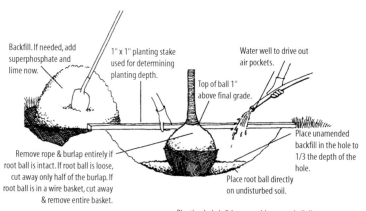

Planting Procedure for Trees and Shrubs

Next remove all twine, rope, and as much of the burlap as possible. Synthetic burlap or other non-degradable materials should be completely removed. If the tree ball is in a wire basket, cut away and remove the top half of the basket.

For plants in containers, inspect the root ball for roots growing in a circle. Correct this situation by freeing and spreading out the roots, roughing up the sides or cutting through the roots in several places.

Stabilize the ball by backfilling the hole. When needed, mix lime and superphosphate (with no additional fertilizer, manure, peat moss, or compost) with the back fill.

A properly staked tree

If you have a windy site, stake the tree now. Trees should not be staked longer than one year because research has shown that staked trees may develop smaller root systems and reduced trunk taper. Two stakes (wood stakes, metal pipes or fence posts) are recommended, one on each side of the trunk but several inches away from it (see drawing above). Protect the trunk by using a flexible tie of some kind, or by slipping wire through a piece of garden hose. Fasten the ties loosely so that the trunk flexes in the wind.

Water the plant thoroughly until the surrounding soil is saturated to the depth of the root ball. Then allow the soil to settle. Resume backfilling and tamp the soil lightly to eliminate air pockets. Do not "pack" the soil too firmly. Compaction will reduce fine air spaces needed for root development.

When planting is completed, water the planting area deeply.

Place mulch to a depth of two to three inches (deeper over lighter soils and shallow over heavy soils) tapering inward, so that no mulch touches the trunk. Mulch piled up against the trunk may promote crown

rot and create a favorable environment for insects. Good mulches are pine bark, aged wood chips, and pine needles.

Caring for Your Plants
— CN

Watering
Frequent watering of your new plants is the most important thing you can do to ensure their survival and growth. Think about how you'll irrigate your garden before you plant it. If you're watering more than a few new plants, some type of drip or micro-irrigation is a good investment. Slow application of water is best, which allows the water to percolate into the soil and wet the top several inches of it. Applying water too fast will result in much of it running off where it is of no benefit to your plants.

New plantings will need water at least twice a week, and you shouldn't depend on turf irrigation systems to provide the right amount of water for annuals or trees and shrubs. Either the turf will be over-watered or the ornamentals under-watered. Sandy, well-drained soils will need to be watered more often than loam soils.

Annuals
Bedding plants need the most frequent watering because their root systems are very limited. In the hot summer, some annuals will need daily watering, others every two to four days. Water when you see signs of wilting, applying enough water to wet the soil to a depth of six to eight inches.

Plants growing in containers need almost daily watering in the heat of summer. The water must drain freely from the drainage holes. A good-quality, well-drained potting mix is essential to prevent root rot.

Perennials
Water deeply every few days until the plants are established, which takes about three to six weeks. After that, water only when the plants need it (they wilt or the soil dries to a depth of two to three inches). How frequent that is depends on soil type, temperatures,

rainfall, and what types of perennials you have. Many perennials die from over-watering, especially where automatic irrigation systems come on a few minutes every day, literally rotting the plants.

Small Trees and Shrubs

Water trees and shrubs thoroughly once or twice a week for the first growing season, or whenever the soil dries out at a one to two inch depth. Apply about 10 gallons of water each time for a 24-inch root ball. Rainfall of more than one-half inch can substitute for watering, but rainfall in smaller amounts doesn't count.

Container-grown plants dry out relatively quickly and will initially need more frequent watering than field-grown plants. Watering frequency can be reduced towards the end of the first growing season, once hot summer weather has passed and roots have begun to grow out into the surrounding soil. Most small shrubs and trees of one-inch diameter or less will be well established and able to grow without much supplemental watering the following season. Larger trees, however, need care for another three years.

Fertilizing

If you have questions about which fertilizer product is best for your garden, ask one of the gardening specialists at the garden center or nursery where you bought your plants.

Annuals and Perennials

For annuals in cool spring weather, an application of a liquid starter fertilizer high in phosphorus (such as 5-15-5) may be beneficial soon after planting. Supplemental soluble fertilizer such as 20-20-20 can be applied to annuals in mid-summer if they need a boost. If fertilizer was added at planting time, perennials generally don't need more during the growing season, unless they show signs of yellowing or slow growth.

Container gardens can be fertilized every seven to 14 days with a soluble fertilizer (such as Miracle Gro™) or with fish emulsion. Alternatively, a three-to-four-month, slow-release fertilizer such as

Osmocote™ could be mixed with the potting soil at planting, or applied to the surface afterwards.

Small Trees and Shrubs

Fertilize new trees and shrubs sparingly, if at all, during the first growing season. A plant with a limited root system isn't able to take up large amounts of nutrients. The growth of roots into the surrounding soil depends largely on stores of energy that the plant accumulated before it was transplanted. In fact, excess fertilizer salts can inhibit rooting (avoid this by using an organic fertilizer). For spring plantings, a fall fertilizer application after the first growing season will provide needed resources for strong growth the next spring.

Weeding and Mulching

Weeds are the bane of many new plantings, and can quickly overgrow small ornamental plants. Pull small weeds often until the plants are large enough to compete. Landscape edging can prevent grasses and other perennial weeds from invading via roots and underground stems. Landscape fabric can be put down before planting landscaped areas (other than annuals) to help suppress weeds. The fabric is porous and unlike plastic allows water penetration and air exchange.

Mulch is very beneficial to new plantings if applied properly. However, mulching too deeply can be fatal to the plants you are trying to protect. Apply two to three inches of organic mulch, such as shredded pine bark or nuggets, pine needles, or shredded leaves, over the entire planting bed for perennials, shrubs and trees. If mulching single trees or shrubs, mulch to the drip line or beyond. Use only an inch of fine-textured mulch on bedding plants, or leave the soil bare. Keep the mulch a few inches away from the stems or trunks of all plants, however, to prevent stem rot and rodent feeding.

Pruning and Deadheading

It isn't necessary or desirable to cut back the top of trees or shrubs at planting—remove only dead, injured, pest-infested, or crossing branches at this time. If a co-dominant stem is present on a tree, cut it back several inches to subdue its growth. No major structural pruning should be done until the second year.

Keeping as much leaf area on the plant as possible provides energy for root growth, the primary goal the first year.

Certain annuals, perennials, and shrubs will benefit from the removal of spent flowers or "deadheads," but in most cases it is not necessary unless they are unsightly. Removing spent blooms can encourage re-bloom on certain plants (roses, for example), or can increase the number of flowers the following year, such as lilacs.

Pest Control

Become familiar with which insects and diseases commonly attack the types of plants you have installed, and what time of year those pests are active. Monitor your plants closely for insects, mites, and disease symptoms, keeping in mind that many beneficial insects may also be present on your plants. When you find diseases or potential pest insects, identify them and decide what kind of control is appropriate. Depending on the pest, it may be best to hand pick them off, prune infested branches, wash with a stream of water, change irrigation practices, or treat with a low-toxicity spray such as soap or oil. For assistance, call the UNH Cooperative Extension's Family, Home, and Garden Education Center toll-free at 1-877-398-4769 or ask someone at your local garden center (visit the New Hampshire Plant Growers' Association Web site at www.nhplantgrowers.org to find a retailer near you).

Fall Preparation and Winter Protection

Tender annuals should be removed in the fall and replaced with hardy annuals or the ground left fallow. Even the hardy annuals usually succumb to a freeze by late November, and should then be removed. A few, such as pansies, will overwinter in mild years if they're mulched.

It's best to cut back most perennials when foliage dies back in late fall, especially large-leafed plants that are matted to the ground. Others with strong, erect stems, such as grasses, *Rudbeckia*, and sedum, can be left standing for a wonderful winter effect.

New perennial gardens and marginally hardy plants need extra winter protection, such as evergreen boughs, pine needles, or salt marsh hay applied thickly in late November (after the ground freezes). Mulch helps reduce alternate freezing and thawing of the soil, which can heave new plants out of the ground. If you apply a thick layer of mulch for winter protection, don't forget to remove it early in the spring.

Evergreen shrubs in locations exposed to winter sun and wind are subject to winter burn if not given some extra protection. Planting on the north and east side of a house usually is adequate to prevent winter burn. For other plants, construct a cage of some type, such as chicken wire or a stake-and-burlap enclosure around the plant, then fill it with leaves. Other methods include placing protective wood shelters over small plants to protect them from direct afternoon sun and strong wind. Make sure all plants, especially evergreens, are well-watered until the ground freezes.

Overwintering shrubs in containers requires special effort to prevent root death from sub-freezing temperatures. One method is simply to remove the plant from the container and plant it in the ground in September or early October. If you want to save the plant to put it back in a container next year, wrap the root ball in a large plastic bag, perforate it for drainage, soak it well, then bury the root ball in the ground. If the tops are marginally hardy, mulch them heavily with leaves as deeply as possible. Another method would be to remove the dormant plant from the pot and store it in an unheated garage. In this case, an insulating layer of something like styrofoam can be laid underneath, the root ball placed into a perforated plastic bag, and both the roots and shoots surrounded with several inches of leaves or other insulating material.

Long-Term Care

Perennials and trees and shrubs are permanent additions to the landscape and need long-term maintenance. Once established, their irrigation needs decrease but chores such as pruning trees or dividing perennials are occasionally necessary to keep plants vigorous and healthy.

Perennials

Continue to fertilize perennials annually in the spring, and again later in the summer for later-blooming varieties or if indicated by signs of reduced vigor or yellow leaves.

Clump-forming perennials may need division every three to five years. Good times for dividing are early spring or in the fall when the leaves start to die back.

Small Trees and Shrubs

Fertilize annually with 24-8-16, 18-6-12, or an organic 5-3-4 slow-release fertilizer in spring or early summer. Another application of nitrogen fertilizer made after leaves color up in fall will enhance growth the following spring. Your garden center specialist can tell you which product is best for your plantings.

Mulch is important for suppressing weeds, conserving water, moderating soil temperatures, and protecting the base of the plants from lawn mowers, weed-eaters, and other injuries. Mulched areas around specimen trees and shrubs should be enlarged each year to allow for optimum growth. When renewing mulch, do not add to the recommended two-to-three-inch depth.

Proper pruning is an art and a science. Learn how to make the right kind of cuts that do not harm the plant. In most cases, selective, natural-form pruning is healthier and more attractive than shearing or indiscriminate pruning.

For more information on watering, fertilizing, and pruning trees and shrubs, look for the following University of New Hampshire Cooperative Extension fact sheets, available from its Family, Home, and Garden Education Center or on the Web at http://ceinfo.unh.edu :

Fertilizing Trees and Shrubs
Using Water Efficiently in the Landscape
Pruning Evergreens in the Home Landscape
Pruning Shade Trees in the Home Landscape
Pruning Deciduous Shrubs in the Home Landscape

Or check with a specialist at your local garden center for information. Visit the New Hampshire Plant Growers' Web site at www.nhplantgrowers.org to find a retailer near you.

Part III

Ways to Use Plants in Your Garden and Landscape

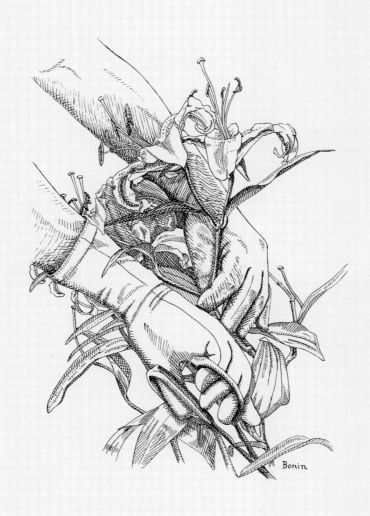

Please consult with your garden center specialist for additional advice on plants listed in this section. Because of space limitations, some plants listed here were not included in preceding sections.

ATTRACTIVE TO BIRDS AND BUTTERFLIES

Annuals
Bachelor's Button (*Centaurea cyanus*)
Blanket Flower (*Gaillardia pulchella*)
Blood Flower (*Asclepias curassavica*)
Brazilian Vervain (*Verbena bonaricnsis*)
Candytuft (*Iberis amara*)
Cleome, Spider Flower (*Cleome hasslerana*)
Common Mignonette (*Reseda odorata*)
Cosmos (*Cosmos bipinnatus*)
Four-o'Clock (*Mirabilis jalapa*)
Fuchsia (*Fuchsia* hybrids*)
Heliotrope (*Heliotropium arborescens*)
Honeywort (*Cerinthe major*)
Lace Flower (*Ammi majus*)
Lantana (*Lantana camara*)
Mexican Sunflower (*Tithonia rotundifolia*)
Morning Glory (*Ipomoea purpurea*)
Nasturtium (*Tropaeolum majus*)
Nicotiana, Flowering Tobacco (*Nicotiana sylvestris*)
Pentas, Star Cluster (*Pentas lanceolata*)
Scarlet Runner Bean (*Phaseolus coccineus*)
Snapdragon (*Antirrhinum majus*)
Sunflower (*Helianthus annuus*)
Sweet Alyssum (*Lobularia maritima*)
Sweet Scabiosa (*Scabiosa atropurpurea*)

Perennials
Anise Hyssop (*Agastache*)
Balloon Flower (*Platycodon*)
Bearded Tongue (*Penstemon*)
Beebalm (*Monarda*)
Bellflower (*Campanula*)
Black-Eyed Susan (*Rudbeckia*)
Butterfly Weed (*Asclepias*)
Candytuft (*Iberis*)
Cardinal Flower (*Lobelia*)
Checker-Mallow (*Sidalcea*)
Columbine (*Aquilegia*)
Coral Bells (*Heuchera*)
Daylily (*Hemerocallis*)

Forget-Me-Not (*Myosotis*)
Foxglove (*Digitalis*)
Gayfeather (*Liatris*)
Iris (*Iris*)
Joe Pye Weed (*Eupatorium*)
Larkspur (*Delphinium*)
Lavender (*Lavandula*)
Lupine (*Lupinus*)
Obedient Plant (*Physostegia*)
Oregano (*Origanum*)
Ornamental Catmint (*Nepeta*)
Ornamental Onion (*Allium*)
Phlox (*Phlox*)
Pincushion Flower (*Scabiosa*)
Pinks (*Dianthus*)
Purple Coneflower (*Echinacea*)
Sage (*Salvia*)
Speedwell (*Veronica*)
Sunflower Heliopsis (*Heliopsis*)
Thrift (*Armeria*)
Tickseed (*Coreopsis*)
Yarrow (*Achillea*)

Small Trees & Shrubs
Amur Maple (*Acer ginnala*)
Arrowwood Viburnum (*Viburnum dentatum*)
Azaleas (*Rhododendron* species and hybrids)
Bearberry (*Arctostaphylus uva-ursi*)
Corneliancherry Dogwood (*Cornus mas*)
Cranberry Cotoneaster (*Cotoneaster apiculatus*)
Doublefile Viburnum (*Viburnum plicatum* var. *tomentosum*)
Flowering Cherry (*Prunus* species and hybrids)
Flowering Crabapple (*Malus* hybrids)
Highbush Blueberry (*Vaccinium corymbosum*)
Inkberry (*Ilex glabra*)
Japanese Tree Lilac (*Syringa reticulata*)
Lowbush Blueberry (*Vaccinium angustifolium*)
Nannyberry Viburnum (*Viburnum lentago*)
Northern Bayberry (*Myrica pensylvanica*)
Red-Twigged Dogwood, Redosier Dogwood (*Cornus sericea*)
Serviceberry, Shadbush (*Amelanchier* species)
Sumac (*Rhus* species)

Summersweet Clethra (*Clethra alnifolia*)
Virginia Creeper (*Parthenocissus quinquefolia*)
White Fringetree (*Chionanthus virginicus*)
Weigela (*Weigela florida*)
Winterberry (*Ilex verticillata*)

AUTUMN COLOR

Perennials
Autumn Fern (*Dryopteris*)
Barrenwort (*Epimedium*)
Blue Star (*Amsonia*)
Bowman's Root (*Gillenia*)
Carolina Phlox (*Phlox maculata*)
Cinquefoil (*Potentilla tridentata*)
Cushion Spurge (*Euphorbia*)
Evening Primrose (*Oenothera*)
Flame Grass (*Miscanthus purascens*)
Hardy Geranium (*Geranium*)
Masterwort (*Astrantia*)
Patrinia
Pigsqueak (*Bergenia*)
Plumbago (*Ceratostigma*)

Small Trees & Shrubs
American Cranberrybush Viburnum (*Viburnum trilobum*)
Amur Maple (*Acer ginnala*)
Arrowwood Viburnum (*Viburnum dentatum*)
Bearberry (*Arctostaphylos ura-ursi*)
Black Tupelo (*Nyssa sylvatica*)
Common Witchhazel (*Hamamelis virginiana*)
Cranberry Cotoneaster (*Cotoneaster apiculatus*)
Doublefile Viburnum (*Viburnum plicatum* var. *tomentosum*)
Fothergilla (*Fothergilla* species)
Fragrant Sumac (*Rhus aromatica*)
Highbush Blueberry (*Vaccinium corymbosum*)
Japanese Maple (*Acer palmatum*)
Kousa Dogwood (*Cornus kousa*)
Lowbush Blueberry (*Vaccinium angustifolium*)
Oakleaf Hydrangea (*Hydrangea quercifolia*)
Red Chokeberry (*Aronia arbutifolia*)
Redvein Enkianthus (*Enkianthus campanulatus*)

Rockspray Cotoneaster (*Cotoneaster horizontalis*)
Royal Azalea (*Rhododendron schlippenbachii*)
Saltspray Rose (*Rosa rugosa*)
Serviceberry or Shadbush (*Amelanchier* species)
Smokebush (*Cotinus coggygria*)
Smooth Sumac (*Rhus glabra*)
Spirea cultivars (*Spiraea japonica*)
Vernal Witchhazel (*Hamamelis vernalis*)
Virginia Creeper (*Parthenocissus quinquefolia*)
Virginia Sweetspire (*Itea virginia*)

CASCADING PLANTS

Annuals
Baby Blue Eyes *(Nemophila menziesii)*
Bacopa *(Sutera cordata)*
Bidens *(Bidens ferulifolia)*
Brachyscome, Swan River Daisy *(Brachyscome iberidifolia)*
Bush Morning Glory (*Convolvulus tricolor)*
Candytuft *(Iberis amara)*
Creeping Zinnia *(Sanvitalia procumbens)*
Diascia, Twinspur *(Diascia barberae)*
Garden Verbena *(Verbena* hybrid*s)*
Ivy Geranium *(Pelargonium peltatum)*
Licorice Plant *(Helichrysum petiolare)*
Lobelia, Edging Lobelia *(Lobelia erinus)*
Million Bells *(Calibrachoa* hybrid*s)*
Moss Rose *(Portulaca grandiflora)*
Nasturtum *(Tropaelum majus)*
Ornamental Sweet Potato *(Ipomoea batatas)*
Petunia *(Petunia* hybrid*s)*
Scaevola, Fan Flower *(Scaevola aemula)*
Sweet Alyssum *(Lobularia maritima)*

Perennials
Artemisia 'Silver Brocade' *(Artemesia stelleriana)*
Aster *(Aster)*
Baby's Breath *(Gypsophila)*
Baltic Ivy *(Hedera helix)*
Barren Strawberry *(Waldsteinia)*
Basket of Gold *(Aurinia)*
Bellflower *(Campanula* 'Poscharskyana')*

Bugleweed (*Ajuga*)
Canadian Phlox (*Phlox divaricata*)
Candytuft (*Iberis*)
Corydalis
Creeping Jenny (*Lysimachia nummularia* 'Aurea'*)*
Creeping Phlox (*Phlox stolonifera*)
Crowberry (*Empetrum nigsum*)
Foam Flower (*Tiarella cordifolia*)
Hens and Chicks (*Sempervivum*)
Lady's Mantle (*Alchemilla*)
Lamb's Ears (*Stachys*)
Moss Phlox (*Phlox subulata*)
Periwinkle (*Vinca minor*)
Saxifrage (*Saxifraga*)
Snow-in-Summer (*Cerastium*)
Stonecrop, low varieties (*Sedum*)
Strawberry (*Fragaria*)
Sweet Woodruff (*Galium*)
Thyme (*Thymus*)
Wintergreen (*Gaultheria*)
Yellow Archangel (*Lamiastrum*)

Small Trees & Shrubs
American Cranberry (*Vaccinium macrocarpon*)
Bearberry (*Arctostaphylos*)
Japanese Garden Juniper (*Juniperus procumbens*)
Rockspray Cotoneaster (*Cotoneaster horizontalis*)
Rose (selected *Rosa* species or hybrids)

CLIMBING PLANTS AND VINES

Annuals
Black-Eyed Susan Vine *(Thunbergia alata)*
Canary Creeper *(Tropaeolum peregrinum)*
Climbing Snapdragon *(Asarina scandens)*
Common Morning Glory *(Ipomoea purpurea)*
Cup-and-Saucer Vine *(Cobaea scandens)*
English Ivy *(Hedera helix)*
Hyacinth Bean *(Dolichos lablab)*
Japanese Hops *(Humulus japonicus)*
Moonflower *(Ipomoea alba)*
Nasturtium *(Tropaeolum majus)*
Ornamental Gourd *(Cucurbita pepo)*
Scarlet Runner Bean *(Phascolus coccineus)*
Spanish Flag *(Ipomoea lobata)*

Star Glory *(Ipomoea quamoclit)*
Sweet Pea *(Lathyrus odoratus)*
Sweet Potato Vine *(Ipomoea batatas)*

Vines
Baltic Ivy (*Hedera helix* 'Baltica')
Boston Ivy (*Parthenocissus tricuspidata*)
Clematis (*Clematis* hybrids)
Climbing Hydrangea (*Hydrangea anomala* subsp. *petiolaris*)
Silver Lace Vine (*Polygonum aubertii*)
Trumpetvine (*Campsis radicans*)
Virginia Creeper (*Parthenocissus quinquefolia*)

DEER-RESISTANT PLANTS

Perennials
If deer are hungry, they'll eat anything. These perennials, however, are less likely to be lunch.
* = repels deer.

Alkanet (*Brunnera*)
Astilbe
Avens (*Geum*)
Baby's Breath (*Gypsophila*)
Balloon Flower (*Platycodon*)
Baltic Ivy (*Hedera*)
Baneberry (*Actaea*)
Barrenwort (*Epimedium*)
Basket of Gold (*Aurinia*)
Bearded Tongue (*Penstemon*)
Beebalm (*Monarda*)
Bellflower (*Campanula*)
Black-Eyed Susan (*Rudbeckia*)
Bleeding Heart (*Dicentra*)
Blue Star (*Amsonia*)
Bolton's Aster (*Boltonia*)
Bugbane (*Cimicifuga*)
Bugleweed (*Ajuga*)
Butterfly Weed (*Asclepias*)
Candytuft (*Iberis*)
Cinquefoil (*Potentilla*)
Columbine (*Aquilegia*)
Coral Bells (*Heuchera*)
Culver's Root (*Veronicastrum*)
Cushion Spurge (*Euphorbia*)
Dead Nettle (*Lamium*)
Evening Primrose (*Oenothera*)
False Blue Indigo (*Baptisia*)
Ferns (many)
Flax (*Linum*)
Foam Flower (*Tiarella*)

Forget-Me-Not (*Myosotis*)
Foxglove (*Digitalis*)
Gas Plant (*Dictamnus*)
Gayfeather (*Liatris*)
Globe Thistle (*Echinops*)
Goatsbeard (*Aruncus*)
Golden Marguerite (*Anthemis*)
Goldenrod (*Solidago*)
Grasses (many)*
Hardy Geranium (*Geranium*)
Iris (sometimes eaten)
Jacob's Ladder (*Polemonium*)
Joe Pye Weed (*Eupatorium*)
Knautia
Lady's Mantle (*Alchemilla*)
Lamb's Ears (*Stachys*)
Larkspur (*Delphinium*)
Lavender (*Lavandula*)*
Lenten Rose (*Helleborus*)
Lily of the Valley (*Convallaria*)
Lungwort (*Pulmonaria*)
Lupine (*Lupinus*)
Mayapple (*Podophyllum*)
Mazus (*Mazus*)
Michaelmas Daisy (*Aster*)
Moss Phlox (*Phlox subulata*)
Mountain Bluet (*Centaurea*)
Mullein (*Verbascum*)
Obedient Plant (*Physostegia*)
Oregano (*Origanum*)
Ornamental Catmint (*Nepeta*)*
Ornamental Onion (*Allium*)*
Parsnip (*Angelica*)
Partridge Berry (*Mitchella*)
Peony (*Paeonia*)
Periwinkle (*Vinca*)
Pigsqueak (*Bergenia*)
Pincushion Flower (*Scabiosa*)
Pinks (*Dianthus*)
Plumbago (*Ceratostigma*)
Plume Poppy (*Macleaya*)
Poppy (*Papaver*)
Primrose (*Primula*)
Purple Coneflower (*Echinacea*)
Queen of the Prairie (*Filipendula*)
Rodger's Flower (*Rodgersia*)
Russian Sage (*Perovskia*)
Sage (*Salvia*)*
Sea Holly (*Eryngium*)
Sea Lavender (*Limonium*)
Shasta Daisy (*Leucanthemum*)
Speedwell (*Veronica*)
Stonecrop, low types (*Sedum*)
Sweet Woodruff (*Galium*)

Thyme (*Thymus*)*
Tickseed (*Coreopsis*)
Turtlehead (*Chelone*)
Violet, most (*Viola*)
Waxbells (*Kirengeshoma*)
Windflower (*Anemone*)
Wintergreen (*Gaultheria*)
Wolfsbane (*Aconitum*)
Wormwood (*Artemisia*)
Yarrow (*Achillea*)*

Small Trees & Shrubs
Bearberry (*Arctostaphylus uva-ursi*)
Boxwood (*Buxus microphylla*)
Callery Pear (*Pyrus calleryana*)
Chinese Juniper (*Juniperus chinensis*)
Clematis (*Clematis* hybrids)
Colorado Spruce (*Picea pungens*)
Cotoneaster (*Cotoneaster* species)
Forsythia (*Forsythia* hybrids)
Inkberry (*Ilex glabra*)
Japanese Pieris (*Pieris japonica*)
Kousa Dogwood (*Cornus kousa*)
Mountain Laurel (*Kalmia latifolia*)
Norway Spruce (*Picea abies*)
Northern Bayberry (*Myrica pensylvanica*)
Periwinkle (*Vinca minor*)
Red-Twigged Dogwood, Redosier Dogwood (*Cornus sericea*)
Redvein Enkianthus (*Enkianthus campanulatus*)
Scotch Heather (*Calluna vulgaris*)
Serviceberry, Shadbush (*Amelanchier* species)
Shrubby Cinquefoil (*Potentilla fruticosa*)
Smokebush (*Cotinus coggygria*)
Spirea (*Spiraea* species)
Spring Heath (*Erica carnea*)
Summersweet Clethra (*Clethra alnifolia*)
White Spruce (*Picea glauca*)

DROUGHT-TOLERANT PLANTS
Annuals
African Daisy (*Dimorphotheca sinuata*)
Ageratum, Flossfower (*Ageratum houstonianum*)
Amaranthus, Love-Lies-Bleeding (*Amaranthus caudatus*)
Annual Baby's Breath (*Gypsophila elegans*)

Annual Phlox (*Phlox drummondii*)
Bachelor's Button (*Centaurea cyanus*)
Blackfoot Daisy (*Melampodium paludosum*)
Border Pink (*Dianthus chinensis*)
Brachyscome, Swan River Daisy (*Brachyscome iberidifolia*)
California Poppy (*Eschscholtzia californica*)
Chinese Forget-Me-Not (*Cynoglossum amabile*)
Cleome, Spider Flower (*Cleome hasslerana*)
Cosmos (*Cosmos bipinnatus*)
Creeping Zinnia (*Sanvitalia procumbens*)
Dusty Miller (*Senecio cineraria*)
Four-O'Clock (*Mirabilis jalapa*)
Garden Verbena (*Verbena* hybrids)
Gloriosa Daisy (*Rudbeckia hirta*)
Greater Periwinkle (*Vinca major* 'Variegata')
Madagascar Periwinkle (*Catharanthus roseus*)
Marguerite (*Argyranthemum* hybrids)
Marigold (*Tagetes* species)
Mexican Sunflower (*Tithonia rotundifolia*)
Morning Glory, Moonflower (*Ipomoea* species)
Moss Rose (*Portulaca grandiflora*)
Narrow-Leaved Zinnia (*Zinnia angustifolia*)
Nasturtium (*Tropaeolum majus*)
Nicotiana, Flowering Tobacco (*Nicotiana alata*)
Perilla (*Perilla frutescens*)
Petunia (*Petunia* hybrids)
Pimpernel (*Anagallis monellii*)
Pot Marigold (*Calendula officinalis*)
Quaking Grass (*Briza maxima*)
Red Sage Lantana (*Lantana camara*)
Snow-on-the-Mountain (*Euphorbia marginata*)
Statice (*Limonium sinuatum*)
Strawflower (*Helichrysum bracteatum*)
Trailing Lantana (*Lantana montevidensis*)

Perennials
Alkanet (*Brunnera*)
Anise Hyssop (*Agastache*)
Baby's Breath (*Gypsophila*)
Balloon Flower (*Platycodon*)

Barren Strawberry (*Waldsteinia*)
Barrenwort (*Epimedium*)
Basket of Gold (*Aurinia*)
Bellflower (*Campanula*)
Bitterroot (*Lewisia*)
Black-Eyed Susan (*Rudbeckia*)
Blue-Eyed Mary (*Omphalodes*)
Butterfly Weed (*Asclepias*)
Calamint (*Calamintha*)
Candytuft (*Iberis*)
Chamomile (*Chamaemelum*)
Cinquefoil (*Potentilla*)
Coral Bells (*Heuchera villosa*)
Cornflower (*Centaurea*)
Creeping Phlox (*Phlox stolonifera*)
Crowberry (*Empetrum*)
Daylily (*Hemerocallis*)
Dead Nettle (*Lamium*)
Evening Primrose (*Oenothera*)
False Blue Indigo (*Baptisia*)
Fescue (*Festuca*)
Foam Flower (*Tiarella*)
Foxglove (*Digitalis*)
Fringed Bleeding Heart (*Dicentra exima*)
Germander (*Teucrium*)
Globeflower (*Trollius*)
Globe Thistle (*Echinops*)
Golden Marguerite (*Anthemis*)
Goldenrod (*Solidago*)
Hardy Geranium (*Geranium*)
Hayscented Fern (*Dennstaedtia*)
Heron's Bill (*Erodium*)
Hosta (*Hosta*)
Hyssop (*Hyssopus*)
Lady's Mantle (*Alchemilla*)
Lamb's Ears (*Stachys*)
Lavender (*Lavandula*)
Lily of the Valley (*Convallaria*)
Lily Turf (*Liriope*)
Lungwort (*Pulmonaria*)
Mallow (*Malva*)
Moss Phlox (*Phlox subulata*)
Oregano (*Origanum*)
Ornamental Catmint (*Nepeta*)
Periwinkle (*Vinca*)
Pincushion Flower (*Scabiosa*)
Pinks (*Dianthus*)
Purple Coneflower (*Echinacea*)
Rock Cress (*Arabis*)
Rue (*Ruta*)
Russian Sage (*Perovskia*)
Sage (*Salvia*)
Sea Holly (*Eryngium*)

Sea Lavender (*Limonium*)
Snow-in-Summer (*Cerastium*)
Soapwort (*Saponaria*)
Solomon's Seal (*Polygonatum*)
Spurge (*Euphorbia*)
Stonecrop (*Sedum*)
Sunflower Heliopsis (*Heliopsis*)
Sweet Woodruff (*Galium*)
Thrift (*Armeria*)
Thyme (*Thymus*)
Tickseed (*Coreopsis*)
Violet (*Viola*)
Winter Savory (*Satureja*)
Wormwood (*Artemisia*)
Yarrow (*Achillea*)
Yellow Archangel (*Lamiastrum*)
Yellow Coneflower (*Ratibida*)

Small Trees & Shrubs
Arborvitae (*Thuja occidentalis*)
Arrowwood Viburnum (*Viburnum dentatum*)
Bearberry (*Arctostaphylos uva-ursi*)
Blackhaw Viburnum (*Viburnum prunifolium*)
Cranberry Cotoneaster (*Cotoneaster apiculatus*)
Common Ninebark (*Physocarpus opulifolius*)
Forsythia (*Forsythia* x *intermedia*)

Fragrant Sumac 'Gro-Low' (*Rhus aromatica*)
Juniper (most *Juniperus* species)
Lilac (*Syringa* species)
Lowbush Blueberry (*Vaccinium angustifolium*)
Nannyberry Viburnum (*Viburnum lentago*)
Northern Bayberry (*Myrica pensylvanica*)
Peashrub (*Caragana arborescens*)
Privet (*Ligustrum* species)
Russian Arborvitae (*Microbiota decussata*)
Saltspray Rose (*Rosa rugosa*)
Shrubby Cinquefoil (*Potentilla fruticosa*)
Smokebush (*Cotinus coggygria*)
Smooth Sumac (*Rhus glabra*)
Spirea cultivars (*Spiraea* species and hybrids)
Summersweet Clethra (*Clethra alnifolia*)

Sweetfern (*Comptonia peregrina*)
Trumpetvine (*Campsis radicans*)
Wayfaringtree Viburnum (*Viburnum lantana*)

EDGING PLANTS
Annuals
Ageratum, Floss Flower (*Ageratum houstonianum*)
Annual Phlox (*Phlox drummondii*)
Baby Blue Eyes (*Nemophila menziesii*)
Blue Daisy (*Felicia amelloides*)
Border Pink (*Dianthus chinensis*)
Brachyscome, Swan River Daisy (*Brachyscome iberidifolia*)
Candytuft (*Iberis umbellata*)
Cockscomb (*Celosia* species)
Creeping Zinnia (*Sanvitalia procumbens*)
Dusty Miller (*Senecio cineraria*)
English Daisy (*Bellis perennis*)
Felicia (*Felicia amelliodes*)
French Marigold (*Tagetes patula*)
Garden Impatiens (*Impatiens walleriana*)
Garden Pansy (*Viola x wittrockiana*)
Garden Verbena (*Verebena* hybrids)
Gazania (*Gazania* hybrids)
Lobelia, Edging Lobelia (*Lobelia erinus*)
Madagascar Periwinkle (*Catharanthus roseus*)
Moss Rose (*Portulaca grandiflora*)
Narrow-Leaved Zinnia (*Zinnia angustifolia*)
Nasturtium (*Tropaeolum majus*)
Petunia (*Petunia* hybrids)
Pimpernel (*Anagallis monellii*)
Quaking Grass (*Briza maxima*)
Scarlet Sage (*Salvia splendens*)
Signet Marigold (*Tagetes tenuifolia*)
Snapdragon (*Antirrhinum majus*)
Sweet Alyssum (*Lobularia maritima*)
Tuberous Begonia (*Begonia x tuberhybrida*)
Wallflower (*Cheiranthus cheri*)
Wax Begonia (*Begonia semperflorens*)
Zinnia (*Zinnia elegans,* dwarf)

Perennials
Alkanet (*Brunnera*)
Astilbe 'Pumila'
Avens (*Geum*)

Barrenwort (*Epimedium*)
Bitterroot (*Lewisia*)
Blue-Eyed Grass (*Sisyrinchium*)
Candytuft (*Iberis*)
Chamomile (*Chamaemelum*)
Cinquefoil (*Potentilla tridentata*)
Coral Bells (*Heuchera*)
Dead Nettle (*Lamium*)
Dwarf Goatsbeard (*Aruncus aethusifolius*)
Dwarf Lady's Mantle (*Alchemilla erythrosora*)
Germander (*Teucrium*)
Ginger (*Asarum*)
Grasses (some)
Hardy Geranium (*Geranium*)
Heron's Bill (*Erodium*)
Hostas (some)
Lamb's Ears (*Stachys*)
Lily Turf (*Liriope*)
Michaelmas Daisy (*Asters*, short)
Moss Phlox (*Phlox subulata*)
Ornamental Catmint (*Nepeta*)
Pigsqueak (*Bergenia*)
Plumbago (*Ceratostigma*)
Rock Cress (*Arabis*)
Rue (*Ruta*)
Sage (*Salvia*)
Self Heal (*Prunella*)
Speedwell (*Veronica*, dwarfs)
Stonecrop (*Sedum*, low types)
Thrift (*Armeria*)
Thyme (*Thymus*)
Tickseed (*Coreopsis*)
Wormwood (*Artemisia*)

Shrubs
Boxwood (*Buxus microphylla* var. *koreana*)
Japanese Garden Juniper (*Juniperus procumbens*)

FLOWERS FOR CUTTING
Annuals
Ageratum, Floss Flower (*Ageratum houstorianum*)
Bachelor's Button (*Centaurea cyanus*)
Bells of Ireland (*Molluccella laevis*)
Blanket Flower (*Gaillardia pulchella*)
Browallia (*Browallia speciosa*)
Canterbury Bells (*Campanula medium*)
China Aster (*Callistephus chinensis*)
Celosia, Cockscomb (*Celosia* species)

Cleome, Spider Flower (*Cleome hasslerana*)
Cosmos (*Cosmos bipinnatus*)
Dahlia (*Dahlia cultivars*)
Garden Mum (*Chrysanthemum* species)
Gloriosa Daisy (*Rudbeckia hirta*)
Heliotrope (*Heliotropium arborescens*)
Joseph's Coat (*Amaranthus tricolor*)
Larkspur (*Consolida ajacis*)
Lisianthus (*Eustoma grandiflorum*)
Love-in-a-Mist (*Nigella damascena*)
Marguerite (*Chrysanthemem fructescens*)
Mexican Sunflower (*Tithonia rotundifolia*)
Nicotiana, Flowering Tobacco (*Nicotiana alata*)
Painted Tongue (*Salpiglossis sinuata*)
Pot Marigold (*Calendula officinalis*)
Salvia (*Salvia* species)
Snapdragon (*Antirrhinum majus*)
Snow-on-the-Mountain (*Euphorbia marginata*)
Stock (*Matthiola incana*)
Strawflower (*Helichrysum bracteatum*)
Sunflower (*Helianthus annuus*)
White Marguerite (*Chrysanthemum frutescens*)
Zinnia (*Zinnia* species)

Perennials
Anise Hyssop (*Agastache*)
Astilbe
Baby's Breath (*Gypsophila*)
Balloon Flower (*Platycodon*)
Bearded Tongue (*Penstemon*)
Beebalm (*Monarda*)
Bellflower (*Campanula*)
Black-Eyed Susan (*Rudbeckia*)
Bleeding Heart (*Dicentra*)
Blue Star (*Amsonia*)
Bowman's Root (*Gillenia*)
Butterfly Weed (*Asclepias*)
Cardinal Flower (*Lobelia*)
Checker-Mallow (*Sidalcea*)
Columbine (*Aquilegia*)
Coral Bells (*Heuchera*)
Corydalis
False Blue Indigo (*Baptisia*)
False Lupine (*Thermopsis*)
Foxglove (*Digitalis*)
Garden Phlox (*Phlox paniculata*)
Globe Thistle (*Echinops*)

Globeflower (*Trollius*)
Golden Marguerite (*Anthemis*)
Goldenrod (*Solidago*)
Grasses
Helen's Flower (*Helenium*)
Hollyhocks (*Alcea*)
Hosta (*Hosta*)
Hyssop (*Hyssopus*)
Iris (*Iris*)
Jacob's Ladder (*Polemonium*)
Japanese Aster (*Asteromoea*)
Joe Pye Weed (*Eupatorium*)
Lady's Mantle (*Alchemilla*)
Larkspur (*Delphinium*)
Lavender (*Lavandula*)
Lenten Rose (*Helleborus*)
Leopard's Bane (*Doronicum*)
Lily of the Valley (*Convallaria*)
Loosestrife (*Lysimachia*)
Meadow Rue (*Thalictrum*)
Merrybells (*Uvularia*)
Michaelmas Daisy (*Aster*)
Mountain Bluet (*Centaurea*)
Obedient Plant (*Physostegia*)
Ornamental Onion (*Allium*)
Peony (*Paeonia*)
Pigsqueak (*Bergenia*)
Pincushion Flower (*Scabiosa*)
Pinks (*Dianthus*)
Plume Poppy (*Macleaya*)
Primrose (*Primula*)
Russian Sage (*Perovskia*)
Sage (*Salvia*)
Sea Holly (*Eryngium*)
Senna
Single Mum (*Dendranthema*)
Speedwell (*Veronica*)
Spurge (*Euphorbia corollata*)
Stokes Aster (*Stokesia*)
Stonecrop (*Sedum*)
Sunflower Heliopsis (*Heliopsis*)
Sun-Rose (*Helianthemum*)
Tickseed (*Coreopsis*)
Toad Lily (*Tricyrtis*)
Violet (*Viola*)
Yarrow (*Achillea*)

Small Trees & Shrubs
* = cut for fruit or branches rather than flowers
Blue Holly, Meserve Holly (*Ilex* x *meserveae*)*
Flowering Crabapple (*Malus* hybrids)
Flowering Cherry (*Prunus* species and hybrids)

Forsythia (*Forsythia* hybrids)
Harry Lauder's Walking Stick (*Corylus avellana* 'Contorta')*
Hydrangea (*Hydrangea* species)
Lilac (*Syringa* species)
Pussy Willow (*Salix caprea* or *chaenomeloides*)*
Red-Twigged Dogwood, Redosier Dogwood (*Cornus sericea*)*
Rose (*Rosa* species)
Spirea (*Spiraea* species)
Summersweet Clethra (*Clethra alnifolia*)
Tree Peony (*Paeonia suffruticosa*)
Weigela (*Weigela florida*)
Winterberry (*Ilex verticillata*)*

FRAGRANT FLOWERS

Annuals
Ageratum, Floss Flower (*Ageratum houstonianum*)
Common Mignonette (*Reseda odorata*)
Compact Innocence (*Nemesia strumosa* 'Compact Innocence')
Garden Pansy (*Viola x wittrockiana*)
Garden Verbena (*Verbena* hybrids)
Heliotrope (*Heliotropium arborescens*)
Marigold (*Tagetes* species)
Money Plant (*Lunaria annua*)
Moonflower (*Ipomoea alba*)
Nicotiana, Flowering Tobacco (*Nicotiana alata*)
Night Stock (*Matthiola longipetala bicornis*)
Petunia (*Petunia* hybrids)
Snapdragon (*Antirrhinum majus*)
Stock (*Matthiola incana*)
Sweet Alyssum (*Lobularia maritima*)
Sweet Pea (*Lathyrus odoratus*)
Sweet William (*Dianthus barbatus*)

Perennials
Basket of Gold (*Aurinia*)
Bugleweed (*Ajuga*)
Butterfly Weed (*Asclepias*)
Candytuft (*Iberis*)
Creeping Jenny (*Lysimachia*)
Daylily (some *Hemerocallis*)
Gas Plant (*Dictamnus*)
Hollyhocks (*Alcea*)
Hosta 'Royal Standard'
Hosta (*Hosta plantaginea*)
Iris (some)

Lavender (*Lavandula*)
Lily of the Valley (*Convallaria*)
Merrybells (*Uvularia*)
Peony (*Paeonia*)
Phlox
Pinks (*Dianthus*)
Single Mums (*Dendranthema*)
Sweet Woodruff (*Galium*)

Small Trees & Shrubs
Burkwood Daphne (*Daphne* x *burkwoodii*)
Burkwood Viburnum (*Viburnum* x *burkwoodii*)
Fothergilla (*Fothergilla* species)
Judd Viburnum (*Viburnum* x *juddii*)
Koreanspice Viburnum (*Viburnum carlesii*)
Lilac (*Syringa* species)
Mockorange (*Philadelphus* hybrids)
Pinkshell Azalea (*Rhododendron vaseyi*)
Pinxterbloom Azalea (*Rhododendron periclymenoides*)
Rose (*Rosa* species)
Roseshell Azalea (*Rhododendron prinophyllum*)
Royal Azalea (*Rhododendron schlippenbachii*)
Star Magnolia (*Magnolia stellata*)
Summersweet Clethra (*Clethra alnifolia*)
Swamp Azalea (*Rhododendron viscosum*)
Tree Peony (*Paeonia suffruticosa*)
Vernal Witchhazel (*Hamamelis vernalis*)
Virginia Sweetspire (*Itea virginia*)

GROUND COVERS

Annuals
Ageratum, Floss Flower (*Ageratum houstonianum*)
Annual Phlox (*Phlox drummondii*)
Blue Daisy (*Felicia amelloides*)
Brachyscome, Swan River Daisy (*Brachyscome iberidifolia*)
Candytuft (*Iberis* species)
Creeping Zinnia (*Sanvitalia procumbens*)
Garden Impatiens (*Impatiens walleriana*)
Garden Verbena (*Verbena* hybrids)

Lobelia, Edging Lobelia (*Lobelia erinus*)
Moss Rose (*Portulaca grandiflora*)
Narrow-Leaved Zinnia (*Zinnia angustifolia*)
Nasturtium (*Tropaeolum majus*)
Petunia (*Petunia* hybrids)
Scaevola, Fan Flower (*Scaevola aemula*)
Sweet Alyssum (*Lobularia maritima*)
Torenia, Wishbone Flower (*Torenia fournieri*)
Wall Baby's Breath (*Gypsophila muvales*)
Wax Begonia (*Begonia semperflorens*)
Zonal Geranium (*Pelargonium x hortorum*)

Perennials
* = *best for crevices and walkways*
Baby's Breath (*Gypsophila*)*
Baltic Ivy (*Hedera helix*)
Barren Strawberry (*Waldsteinia*)*
Barrenwort (*Epimedium rubrum*)
Basket of Gold (*Aurinia*)*
Bellflower (*Campanula*, low types)*
Big-Root Geranium (*Geranium macrorrhizum*)
Blue-Eyed Mary (*Omphalodes*)
Bugleweed (*Ajuga*)*
Bunchberry (*Cornus canadensis*)
Canada Anemone (*Anemone canadensis*)
Candytuft (*Iberis*)*
Cinquefoil (*Potentilla tridentata*)*
Clover (*Trifolium*)*
Coral Bells (*Heuchera villosa*)
Creeping Phlox (*Phlox stolonifera*)*
Creeping Jenny (*Lysimachia num.* 'Aurea')*
Creeping Wintergreen, Checkerberry (*Gaultheria procumbens*)
Daylily (*Hemerocallis*)
Ferns
Foamflower (*Tiarella*)
Forget-Me-Not (*Myosotis*)*
Goldenrod (*Solidago*)
Grasses
Hawkweed (*Hieracium*)*
Hens and Chicks (*Sempervivum*)*
Heron's Bill (*Erodium*)*
Hosta*
Lady's Mantle (*Alchemilla*)
Lamb's Ears (*Stachys*)*
Mazus*

Ornamental Catmint (*Nepeta* 'Blue
    Wonder')
Ornamental Onion (*Allium senescens*)*
Pearlwort (*Sagina*)*
Periwinkle (*Vinca*)
Pinks (*Dianthus*)*
Plumbago (*Ceratostigma*)*
Rock Cress (*Arabis sturii*)*
Saxifrage (*Saxifraga*)*
Single Mum (*Dendranthema* 'White
    Bomb')*
Snow-in-Summer (*Cerastium*)
Spurge (*Pachysandra*)
Stonecrop (*Sedum*)
Strawberry (*Fragaria*)
Thyme (*Thymus*)*
Wormwood (*Artemisia*)*
Yellow Archangel (*Lamiastrum*)

Small Trees & Shrubs
American Cranberry (*Vaccinium
    macrocarpon*)
Bearberry (*Arctostaphylus uva-ursi*)
Black Crowberry (*Empetrum nigrum*)
Chinese Juniper (*Juniperus chinensis*)
Creeping Juniper (*Juniperus
    horizontalis*)
Fragrant Sumac 'Gro-Low' (*Rhus
    aromatica*)
Greenstem Forsythia (*Forsythia
    viridissima* 'Bronxensis')
Japanese Garden Juniper (*Juniperus
    procumbens*)
Lowbush Blueberry (*Vaccinium
    angustifolium*)
Pachysandra (*Pachysandra terminalis*)
Rockspray Cotoneaster (*Cotoneaster
    horizontalis*)
Russian Arborvitae (*Microbiota
    decussata*)
Savin Juniper (*Juniperus sabina*)
Scotch Heather (*Calluna vulgaris*)
Spring Heath (*Erica carnea*)
Sweetfern (*Comptonia peregrina*)
Virginia Creeper (*Parthenocissus
    quinquefolia*)

HEDGES AND SCREENS

Annuals
Castor Bean (*Ricinus communis*)
Celosia, tall varieties (*Celosia* species)
Cleome, Spider Flower (*Cleome
    hasslerana*)
Cosmos (*Cosmos bipinnatus*)

Elephant's Ear (*Colocasia esculenta*)
Fountain Grass (*Pennisetum setaceum*)
Joseph's Coat (*Amaranthus tricolor*)
Marigold, tall varieties (*Tagetes
    species*)
Mexican Sunflower (*Tithonia*)
Sunflower (*Helianthus annuus*)
Zinnia, tall varieties (*Zinnia elegans*)

Small Trees & Shrubs
American Cranberrybush Viburnum
    (*Viburnum trilobum*)
Amur Maple (*Acer ginnula*)
Anglojap Yew (*Taxus* x *media*)
Arborvitae, White Cedar (*Thuja
    occidentalis*)
Arrowwood Viburnum (*Viburnum
    dentatum*)
Blue Holly, Meserve Holly (*Ilex* x
    meserveae)
Boxwood (*Buxus microphylla*)
Chinese Juniper (*Juniperus chinensis*)
Common Ninebark (*Physocarpus
    opulifolius*)
Corneliancherry Dogwood (*Cornus
    mas*)
Eastern Hemlock (*Tsuga canadensis*)
Hedge Maple (*Acer campestre*)
Inkberry (*Ilex glabra*)
Lilac (*Syringa* species)
Northern Bayberry (*Myrica
    pensylvanica*)
Peashrub (*Caragana* species)
Privet (*Ligustrum* species)
Purpleosier Willow (*Salix purpurea*)
Rocky Mountain Juniper (*Juniperus
    scopulorum*)
Rose (*Rosa* species)
Saltspray Rose (*Rosa rugosa*)
Smooth Sumac (*Rhus glabra*)
Spirea (*Spiraea* x *vanhouttei*)
Wayfaringtree Viburnum (*Viburnum
    lantana*)

OUTSTANDING FOLIAGE

Annuals
Annual Fountain Grass (*Pennisetum
    setaceum*)
Caladium (*Caladium* x *hortulanum*)
Canna (*Canna* x *generalis*)
Castor Bean (*Ricinus communis*)
Coleus (*Solenostemon scutellarioides*)
Dusty Miller (*Senecio cineraria*)
Elephant's Ear (*Colocasia esculenta*)

Hyacinth Bean (*Dolichos lablab*)
Licorice Plant (*Helichrysum petiolare*)
New Guinea Impatiens (*Impatiens*
    hybrid*s*)
Ornamental Sweet Potato (*Ipomoea
    batatas*)
Plectranthus (*Plectranthus* species)
Polka-Dot-Plant (*Hypoestes
    phyllostachya*)
Purple Heart (*Tradescantia pallida*
    'Purpurea')
Swiss Chard (*Beta vulgaris*)

Small Trees & Shrubs
Japanese Maple (*Acer palmatum*)
Willow 'Hakuro Nishiki' (*Salix
    integra* 'Hakuro Nishiki')

POISONOUS PLANTS

*Some of these ornamental landscape
plants may be toxic if they're ingested in
sufficient quantites. Others can cause
dermatitis on people who are sensitive.
Children should be taught not to eat
any plants or plant parts, regardless of
whether or not they're on this list. The
absence of a plant from this list does not
imply that the plant is safe. If poisoning
is suspected, call the National Poison
Information Center at 1-800-222-
1222.*

Annuals
Caladium (*Caladium* x *hortulanum*)
Castor Bean (*Ricinus communis*)
Elephant's Ear (*Colocasia esculenta*)
English Ivy (*Hedera helix*)
Lantana (*Lantana camara*)
Lobelia, Edging Lobelia (*Lobelia
    erinus*)
Morning Glory (*Ipomoea* species)
Pansy (*Viola* x *wittrockiana*)
Sweet Pea (*Lathyrus ordoratus*)

Perennials
Baltic Ivy (*Hedera*)
Bleeding Heart (*Dicentra*)
Bloodroot (*Sanguinaria*)
Butterfly Weed (*Asclepias*)
Cardinal Flower (*Lobelia*)
Checker-Mallow (*Sidalcea*)
Columbine (*Aquilegia*)
Corydalis
Ferns (*Dryopteris*)

Foxglove (*Digitalis*)
Goldenrod (*Solidago*)
Helen's Flower (*Helenium*)
Hollyhocks (*Alcea*)
Iris
Jack in the Pulpit (*Arisaema*)
Larkspur (*Delphinium*)
Lenten Rose (*Helleborus*)
Lily of the Valley (*Convallaria*)
Lupine (*Lupinus*)
Marsh Marigold (*Caltha*)
Meadow Rue (*Thalictum*)
Peony (*Paeonia*)
Periwinkle (*Vinca*)
Poppy (*Papaver*)
Rue (*Ruta*)
Speedwell (*Veronicas*, some)
Spurge (*Euphorbia*)
Stonecrop (*Sedum*)
Windflower (*Anemone*)
Wolfsbane, Monkshood (*Aconitum*)
Wormwood (*Artemisia*)
Yarrow (*Achillea*)

Small Trees & Shrubs
Angel's Trumpet (*Datura* species)
Black Locust (*Robinia pseudoacacia*)
Choke Cherry, Wild Cherry (*Prunus serotina, P. virginiana*)
Daphne (*Daphne* species)
Elderberry (*Sambucus* species)
English Ivy (*Hedera helix*)
Glossy Buckthorne (*Rhamnus frangula*)
Holly (*Ilex* species)
Hydrangea (*Hydrangea* species)
Kentucky Coffeetree (*Gymnocladius dioicus*)
Mountain Laurel (*Kalmia latifolia*)
Ohio Buckeye (*Aesculus glabra*)
Privet (*Ligustrum vulgare*)
Virginia Creeper (*Parthenocissus quinquefolia*)
Wahoo (*Euonymus atropurpureus*)
Wisteria (*Wisteria* species)
Yew (*Taxus* species)

SALT-TOLERANT PLANTS
Annuals
Chrysanthemums (*Chrysanthemum* species)
Cornflower (*Centaurea cyanus*)
Dianthus, Pinks (*Dianthus* species)
Gazania (*Gazania* hybrids)
Gladiolus (*Gladiolus* species)

Petunia (*Petunia* hybrids)
Portulaca (*Portulaca grandiflora*)
Zinnia (*Zinnia* species)

Perennials
* = toughest plants
Alkanet (*Brunnera*)
Astilbe
Balloon Flower(*Platycodon*)
Barrenwort (*Epimedium*)
Basket of Gold (*Aurinia*)
Bleeding Heart (*Dicentra*)
Bugbane (*Cimicifuga*)
Bugleweed (*Ajuga*)
Candytuft (*Iberis*)
Cardinal Flower (*Lobelia*)
Columbine (*Aquilegia*)
Coral Bells (*Heuchera*)
Cushion Spurge (*Euphorbia*)
Daisy (*Chrysanthemum* types)
Daylily (*Hemerocallis**)
False Blue Indigo (*Baptisia**)
Foam Flower (*Tiarella*)
Foxglove (*Digitalis*)
Gas Plant (*Dictamnus*)
Globe Thistle (*Echinops*)
Goldenrod (*Solidago*)
Grasses
Hosta
Iris
Jacob's Ladder (*Polemonium*)
Lamb's Ears (*Stachys**)
Lenten Rose (*Helleborus*)
Lily of the Valley (*Convallaria*)
Lily Turf (*Liriope*)
Meadow Rue (*Thalictrum*)
Michaelmas Daisy (*Asters*)
Montauk Daisy (*Nippothemum*)*
Northern Sea Oat (*Chasmanthium*)
Obedient Plant (*Physostegia*)*
Ornamental Catmint (*Nepeta*)*
Peach-Leafed Bellflower (*Campanula persicifolia*)
Peony (*Paeonia*)
Periwinkle (*Vinca*)
Phlox (*Phlox*)
Pinks (*Dianthus*)
Poppy (*Papaver*)
Primrose (*Primula*)
Sage (*Salvia**)
Sea Holly (*Eryngium*)
Sea Lavender (*Limonium*)
Snow-in-Summer (*Cerastium*)
Speedwell (*Veronica*)

Spurge (*Pachysandra*)
Stonecrop (*Sedum*)
Thrift (*Armeria*)
Thyme (*Thymus*)
Tickseed (*Coreopsis*)
Violet (*Viola*)
Windflower (*Anemone*)
Winter Savory (*Satureja*)
Wormwood (*Artemisia**)
Yarrow (*Achillea*)

Small Trees & Shrubs
Arrowwood Viburnum (*Viburnum dentatum*)
Bearberry (*Arctostaphylus uva-ursi*)
Colorado Spruce (*Picea pungens*)
Crowberry (*Empetrum nigrum*)
Hedge Maple (*Acer campestre*)
Inkberry (*Ilex glabra*)
Juniper (*Juniperus*)
Northern Bayberry (*Myrica pensylvanica*)
Peashrub (*Caragana arborescens*)
Saltspray Rose (*Rosa rugosa*)
Smooth Sumac (*Rhus glabra*)
Virginia Creeper (*Parthenocissus quinquefolia*)
Willow (*Salix*)

SPRING-FLOWERING BULBS
Crocus (*Crocus*)
Daffodils (*Narcissus*)
Garden Hyacinth (*Hyacinthus*)
Grecian Windflower (*Anemone blanda*)
Glory of the Snow (*Chionodoxa*)
Grape Hyacinth (*Muscari*)
Guinea Flowers (*Fritillaria meleagris*)
Ornamental Onions (*Allium*)
Snow Iris (*Iris reticulata*)
Snowdrops (*Galanthus*)
Squills (*Scilla, Puschkinia*)
Trout Lily (*Erythronium*)
Tulips (*Tulipa*)
Winter Aconites (*Eranthis*)

WINTER INTEREST
Perennials
These plants will hold their stems and seed heads through most of the winter.
Astilbe
Black-Eyed Susan (*Rudbeckia*)
Bolton's Aster (*Boltonia*)

Bugbane (*Cimicifuga*)
Butterfly Weed (*Asclepias*)
Canadian Burnet (*Sanguisorba*)
Celandine Poppy (*Stylophorum*)
Culver's Root (*Veronicastrum*)
False Blue Indigo (*Baptisia*)
False Lupine (*Thermopsis*)
Gas Plant (*Dictamnus*)
Globe Thistle (*Echinops*)
Goatsbeard (*Aruncus*)
Goldenrod (*Solidago*)
Grasses
Ligularia
Lily Turf (*Liriope*)
Masterwort (*Astrantia*)
Meadow Rue (*Thalictrum*)
Ornamental Onion (*Allium*)
Pasque Flower (*Pulsatilla*)
Plumbago (*Ceratostigma*)
Purple Coneflower (*Echinacea*)
Queen of the Prairie (*Filipendula*)
Russian Sage (*Perovskia*)
Sea Lavender (*Limonium*)
Senna
Siberian Iris (*Iris sibirica*)
Stonecrop (*Sedum*)
Tickseed (*Coreopsis verticillata*)
Wormwood (*Artemisia lactiflora*)
Yellow Coneflower (*Ratibida*)

Small Trees & Shrubs
Amur Chokecherry (*Prunus maackii*)
Amur Maple (*Acer ginnala*)
Blue Holly, Meserve Holly (*Ilex* x
  meserveae)
Common Ninebark (*Physocarpus
  opulifolius*)
Corneliancherry Dogwood (*Cornus
  mas*)
Flowering Crabapple *(Malus* hybrids)
Japanese Kerria (*Kerria japonica*)
Japanese Stewartia *(Stewartia
  pseudocamellia*)
Kousa Dogwood (*Cornus kousa*)
Paper Birch *(Betula papyrifera*)
Paperbark Maple (*Acer griseum*)
Red-Twigged Dogwood, Redosier
  Dogwood (*Cornus sericea*)
River Birch (*Betula nigra*)
Smooth Sumac (*Rhus glabra*)
Winterberry *(Ilex verticillata*)

Bonin

GLOSSARY

Cultivar: A variety of plant which has arisen or been selected in the course of cultivation. It may be propagated by any means that preserves its distinctive character. A cultivar's name is set off by single quotation marks and follows the species name or genus name. For example, *Acer rubrum* 'Red Sunset.'

Family: A group of genera (*singular,* genus).

*Genus (*plural, *genera):* The taxonomic group between family and species. Genus includes one or more species that have certain characteristics in common.

Hybrid: A crossbred plant that's the offspring of two parents that differ in one or more inheritable characteristics; the offspring of a cross between two different species or varieties.

Species: A population of wild plants which are sufficiently alike to carry the same name, and which will breed freely with one another to give rise to offspring like themselves.

Variety: A subdivision of a species which differs as a group in some minor definable characteristic from the rest of the species.

Bonin

RESOURCES FOR GARDENERS

The New Hampshire Plant Growers' Association

Enter the New Hampshire Plant Growers' Association Web Site at www.nhplantgrowers.org by clicking on "Gardening Enthusiasts" and find out:

- *Where to shop for both indoor and outdoor plants, flowers, trees and shrubs, and gardening products and supplies.* Type in the name of your town to find the NHPGA retailer nearest you.

- *How to cultivate a bountiful garden.* For more information on how to make your garden grow, visit the NHPGA retailer nearest you. And check out these Web sites:

University of New Hampshire Cooperative Extension www.ceinfo.unh.edu

UNH Cooperative Extension's Master Gardener Program www.ceinfo.unh.edu/agmastgd.htm

New Hampshire Farms www.nhfarms.com

Fine Gardening **magazine** www.finegardening.com

The Gardener Magazine www.thegardenermagazine.com

Horticulture Magazine www.hortmag.com

People, Places, and Plants **magazine** www.newenglandgardening.com

Garden Net www.gardennet.com

Perry's Perennial Pages www.uvm.edu/~pass/perry/

New England Wildflower Society www.newfs.org

The Arnold Arboretum of Harvard University www.arboretumharvard.edu

New York Botanical Garden www.nybg.org

Tower Hill Botanic Garden www.towerhillbg.org

American Horticultural Society www.ahs.org

National Gardening Association www.garden.org

- *How to support horticultural research.* The New Hampshire Horticultural Endowment was founded in 1997 by the New Hampshire Plant Growers' Association. It is the only grant maker in New Hampshire that awards funds to individuals engaged in ornamental horticulture research and education. Administered by the New Hampshire Charitable Foundation, the Endowment has awarded grants of $2,500 each year since 1999. For more information, click on "Support Horticultural Research" on the NHPGA Web site www.nhplantgrowers.org or call the NHPGA office at 603 225-0653.

- *About upcoming events for gardeners.* Once you're in the NHPGA Web site, click on "Gardening Events" for up-to-date information about workshops, garden tours, lectures, and more.

- *How to get in touch with the office.* Write to NHPGA at 5 Birch Tree Lane, Bow, NH 03304, e-mail at nhpga@totalnetnh.net, or call 603 225-0653.

UNH Cooperative Extension's Family, Home and Garden Education Center

Located at 200 Bedford Street, Mill #3, Manchester, NH 03101, the Center offers:

- *A toll-free Info Line 1-877-398-4769.* Open Monday–Friday from 9 A.M. to 2 P.M., the Info Line is staffed by trained volunteers who help callers find solutions to everyday garden problems.

- *A walk-in identification clinic.* Clinic staff members identify insect pests, unknown plants, and plant diseases on Tuesday mornings from April to September in Room 293 of the Center. Call the Info Line for hours.

- *Workshop and educational programs.* For details on programs offered throughout the year, check UNH Cooperative Extension's Web site at www.ceinfo.unh.edu.

- *Ongoing community projects and access to hundreds of Home and Garden, Food Preservation and Food Safety informational fact sheets.* These are available on the UNHCE Web site at ceinfo.unh.edu.

UNH Cooperative Extension's Diagnostic Labs

The University's three diagnostic labs, all located on the Durham campus, require gardeners to fill out a form and follow specific instructions for mailing their samples. You can download forms from UNH Cooperative Extension's URLs listed below or call the toll-free Info Line at 1-877-398-4769 to receive them in the mail. Each lab charges a fee for its test.

- *Analytical Services Lab—Soil Testing.* Plants grow best in a soil with balanced nutrition and correct pH. For a form explaining how to prepare and submit a soil sample for testing, call the toll-free Info Line at 1-877-398-4769, or visit http://aslan.unh.edu:80/unhsoiltesting/

- *Plant Diagnostic Lab.* UNH Cooperative Extension plant-health specialists identify plant pathogens, pests, and stress-related disorders, and provide recommendations for management. To download a form with instructions for mailing samples, visit http://ceinfo.unh.edu/Agriculture/Documents/agplhlth.htm

- *Arthropod (Insect and Spider) Identification Center.* The Arthropod Center will identify samples of insects or spiders. Bring or send samples to 117 Spaulding Hall, University of New Hampshire, Durham, NH 03824. To download a form with instructions for mailing samples, visit http://ceinfo.unh.edu/Common/Documents/arthroid.htm For more information, call the toll-free Info Line at 1-877-398-4769 or 862-3200.

UNH Cooperative Extension Master Gardener Program

Since 1993, UNH Cooperative Extension has trained Master Gardeners who share their enthusiasm for gardening with the general public by serving as volunteer educators in their communities. For more information call 1-877-398-4769, or visit http://ceinfo.unh.edu/agmastgd.htm

UNH Cooperative Extension County Offices

Agricultural resources staff in each of the state's county Extension offices help gardeners identify insect and weed pests and plant diseases. Call in advance before bringing your sample to the office.

Belknap
(603) 527-5475

Carroll
(603) 539-3331

Cheshire
(603) 352-4550

Coös
(603) 788-4961

Grafton
(603) 787-6944

Hillsborough
Milford (603) 673-2510
Goffstown, to open in 2004 (603) 621-1478

Merrimack
(603) 225-5505
(603) 796-2151

Rockingham
(603) 679-5616

Strafford
(603) 749-4445

Sullivan
(603) 863-9200

INDEX